The Flammarion engraving is a wood engraving by an unknown artist that first appeared in Camille Flammarion's L'atmosphère: météorologie populaire (1888). The image depicts a man crawling under the edge of the sky, depicted as if it were a solid hemisphere, to look at the mysterious Empyrean beyond.

Physics of the Non-Physical

John Joseph Petrovic

Endorsements

Dr. Dean Radin: Chief Scientist at the Institute of Noetic Sciences

"Physics of the Non-Physical is a clear and scientifically accurate account of an aspect of reality that's been staring us in the face for millennia, but has remained strangely invisible to most scientists. But not to all. Dr. John Petrovic, a scientist from one of the world's most prominent government laboratories, reveals this "other reality" in this engaging and well-written book."

Dr. Pim van Lommel: Cardiologist and Near-Death Experience Researcher

"The most glaring deficiency in our present science is the complete lack of understanding of consciousness. Based on his extensive knowledge and deep insight in quantum physics and string theory, and referring to the overwhelming evidence that at the present time materialist science is only able to describe 5% of our observable physical universe, John Petrovic comes in his impressive and important book *Physics of the Non-Physical* to the inevitable conclusion that consciousness must be the most basic fundamental of reality. Universal consciousness, pervading all things both physical and non-physical, can be conceived as a non-physical energy field, in analogy with the quantum physical zero-point field. We cannot detect consciousness because it exists outside our physical space-time. Highly recommended."

Dedication

This book is dedicated to all those scientists who are willing to read it with an open mind. May it serve as a catalyst to enlarge their view of reality and inspire them to construct new scientific paradigms.

Acknowledgements

My thanks to Hal Puthoff, Russell Targ, Rupert Sheldrake, Dean Radin, and Gary Schwartz for conducting scientific experiments targeted at probing the non-physical. They have served as an inspiration for the present endeavor. The author also wishes to acknowledge his loving wife, Blanche, and our brilliant daughter, Michelle, for moral support and for allowing him to devote the time necessary to make this book a reality.

Table of Contents

Preface

You do not need to be a scientist or have a physics or mathematical background in order to read and understand what I have written in this book. I have put forward the material in a format which is understandable by the non-scientist. There are very few equations in the book. On occasion, I employ scientific notation to conveniently represent numbers that are very small or very large (e.g. $0.000000000002 = 2 \times 10^{-12}$ and $2000000000000 = 2 \times 10^{12}$).

For those of you without much knowledge of science, in these pages you will discover that our current science actually understands relatively little about the physical world which surrounds us, both the vast cosmos and the infinitesimal. It is a fact that at the present time, science is only able to describe 5% of our observable physical universe in terms of existing scientific paradigms. And you will come to appreciate that much of our present science is based upon aspects that are more aptly characterized as metaphysical, or non-physical, in nature.

For those scientists and people with scientific background knowledge, I believe you may find that the science which you think you know has very significant gaps in what it actually knows. The two overarching paradigms of modern science, the theory of relativity and the theory of quantum mechanics, are not able to account adequately for what we observe in our so-called physical realm, from the expanse of the universe to the point singularity of a black hole. The most glaring deficiency in our present science is the complete lack of understanding of consciousness, an attribute that every person knows they have at their most fundamental level. Consciousness is a reality that exists in the non-physical and science must come to terms with it. Only then can science proceed to the next stage of describing the true nature of reality.

Each book section is headed by an appropriate quotation from a famous physicist. In the first half of the book, I outline the various aspects and assumptions that underlie the theories of relativity and quantum mechanics. I think you may be surprised at what really forms the basis for each of these theories. I highlight a number of key issues in physics that have not yet been satisfactorily addressed. In the second half of the book, I direct your attention to phenomena that are presently considered to be non-physical by science. The non-physical phenomena that I discuss are well-documented and are clearly part of our reality. Science neglects or dismisses the existence of these "inconvenient truths" because they cannot be explained by current scientific paradigms, but for science to progress in a meaningful way they must be addressed. Finally, I suggest that consciousness is the overarching fundamental quantity that underlies both the physical and the non-physical. Everything derives from a field of Universal Consciousness that resides in the non-physical realm and which contains the physical realm as a subset.

So prepare yourself for a physical mystery tour and a descent into the black hole. You are about to experience the physics of the non-physical.

The day science begins to study non-physical phenomena, it will make more progress in one decade than in all the previous centuries of its existence. To understand the true nature of the universe, one must think it terms of energy, frequency and vibration.

Nikola Tesla

The Physical and the Non-Physical:

In beginning this book, it is appropriate to ask the question: What is physical and what is non-physical? One might say that the physical is whatever we can detect with our five physical senses or with the scientific instruments which extend the range of our physical senses. Consider the existence of a flower. I can see the flower, touch it, smell it, hear the bees pollinating it, and if I should desire even taste it. This I can do directly with my own personal physical senses.

Now consider something that is invisible to my sight, such as electromagnetic radiation outside the range of visible light. I cannot see it, feel it, smell it, hear it, or taste it, but it still exists in the physical. All sorts of non-visible electromagnetic radiation such as radio and microwaves permeate my body, although I do not feel it physically in a personal way. Yet, I know this radiation exists because of the scientific instruments that can detect it and the effects which this radiation produces on other physical things. Without electromagnetic radiation, we could not use our televisions, radios, or cellphones.

We know that our body is composed of approximately 40 trillion individual cells, although we do not detect these individual cells with our physical senses. Rather, they can be observed with microscopes that extend our physical senses. Similarly, each of these cells contains a DNA molecule in its nucleus which controls the functioning of the cell. While we cannot see this DNA molecule ourselves directly with our eyes, we know it exists because it can be chemically isolated and examined with chemical techniques.

All of the above things are part of the physical, they are part of what we can discern with our senses or with equipment that extends our senses. But are there things that are not detectible in any way by our senses or current instruments? Yes, there are. One such thing is consciousness. Each of us knows that we are conscious, but we are not able to pin down any of the characteristics of this consciousness with our senses or sense-extending scientific devices. From the physical perspective, consciousness does not exist, yet we know it does. Consciousness is non-physical.

We all know that we have an inner life and awareness that is independent of the gross physical inputs of our five senses. We can see a red flower with our eyes, but this has nothing to do with our interpretation of the "redness of red" in our mind. We can hear someone singing a song with our ears, but that does not explain how we can appreciate the beauty of the voice that sings the song. We can smell the aroma and taste food, but this is not associated with our gratitude in having been served a delicious meal. We can touch the skin of our lover, but that touch conveys so much more to us. These are all qualia associated with our non-physical consciousness, our inner life.

Extrasensory perception such as telepathy, clairvoyance, precognition, and telekinesis are examples of phenomena that are considered to be non-physical by our present science. This is because these phenomena cannot be explained by any of our current scientific paradigms. Yet, there is much evidence that demonstrates the true existence of such non-physical things. They occur as a result of mechanisms that are presently considered non-physical in nature. The same can be said for phenomena such as near-death and out-of-body experiences. There is a large body of well-documented evidence that phenomena like extrasensory perception and out-of-body experiences actually do exist, but their operative mechanisms are non-physical.

One might say that things like so-called Dark Matter and Dark Energy are of a non-physical nature. Science presently says that Dark Matter and Dark Energy make up 95% of our physical universe. Dark Matter has an effect on the velocities of stars in galaxies and Dark Energy has an effect on the expansion rate of the universe. However, science has been unable to physically establish direct descriptional evidence for either Dark Matter and Dark Energy. Indeed, this is the reason that science has named them by employing the preface word "Dark". These phenomena are considered to be non-physical at the present time.

Clearly, there are a great many things that can be defined as non-physical in our physical world. I have written this book in order to explore as far as one can the physics of these non-physical phenomena. Are such things metaphysical? Metaphysics means "beyond physics", and is defined as the branch of philosophy exploring the fundamental nature of reality. I think that what is being presented in this book does indeed venture into metaphysics in the sense that new scientific paradigms must be considered.

The important thing in science is not so much to obtain new facts as to discover new ways of thinking about them.

William Bragg

Current Overarching Theories of Physics:

Physics is the subset of science that deals with explaining the basis of physical reality. The 20th century saw the development of two major scientific paradigms that continue to shape the framework of physics in the 21st. These two paradigms are the theory of relativity and the theory of quantum mechanics. The first describes the behavior of the vast cosmos, while the second describes the behavior of the smallest pieces of matter and energy.

In the year 1905 Einstein published his famous theory of special relativity. It postulated a number of truly revolutionary concepts in physics. Prior to the publication of his theory, physicists conceived that there was a fixed, absolute frame of reference through which everything in the universe – the Earth, the Moon, the Planets, the Sun, the Milky Way galaxy – moved. Everything was contained in this three-dimensional framework, which was called the aether. Furthermore, light was a wave that propagated through the aether and the speed of light was dictated by the wave propagation velocity in the medium of the aether. This view implied that an observer's measurement of the speed of light should change depending on the direction it was measured with respect to the direction that the Earth was moving through the aether.

However, when the physicists Michelson and Morley conducted a key experiment with light in 1887, they observed that the speed of light was constant in every direction of measurement regardless of the direction the Earth was moving in the postulated aether. This lead a number of physicists to begin surmising that perhaps there was no aether, that the aether did not exist. But the absence of the aether left a conceptual "vacuum" in the world of physics.

This was the quandary that physics found itself faced with in the year 1905 when Einstein published his revolutionary paper on special relativity. What Einstein put forth was profound. There was no aether. Aether did not exist. Instead, Einstein postulated that the speed of light was a constant in all observational frames of reference. This assumption required that the previously considered independent concepts of space and time be melded together into a new quantity called spacetime. The special theory of relativity indicated that observations of space and time depend on the relative motions of the observer and the observed object. Furthermore, the speed of light is a constant of the universe. Nothing can travel faster than light. Light is an absolute cosmic speed limit. Oh, and by the way, it also predicted that matter was equivalent to energy, $E = mc^2$.

In 1916, Einstein published his general theory of relativity. This was a more general formalism than special relativity which incorporated the effects of gravity that influence cosmic bodies. Einstein's general theory said that, instead of three-dimensional space and independent time, the fabric of the universe was actually a four-dimensional spacetime. Furthermore, large mass bodies in space had the effect of distorting spacetime and it was this distortion that produced the effects that we call gravity. Thus, matter traveling through space would be attracted to other pieces of matter as a result of this distortion. In effect, the gravitational field attraction between two objects of mass was really a distortion of spacetime. In addition, such effects also applied to electromagnetic waves such as light. Their travel through space would also be similarly affected. Einstein's general theory predicted that light rays would be "bent" when they traveled close to a large body in space such as a star.

Needless to say, Einstein's theory of relativity was so revolutionary that physicists at the time found it difficult to accept as reality. However, in 1919 the astrophysicist Arthur Eddington traveled to Africa to study a total eclipse of the sun that could be observed there. What Eddington saw during the eclipse was that stars near the eclipsed disc of the sun appeared to be shifted in their positions. This meant the light from these stars was indeed being bent as it traveled near the sun, an observation that dramatically verified Einstein's prediction. As a consequence of this result, Einstein's theory of relativity became widely accepted by the scientific community.

Einstein's theory of relativity makes some rather startling predictions about the nature of reality. The first is that reality has a fundamentally relative nature. This means that what we observe depends on how we are moving in spacetime in relation to how the object we are observing is moving. One unusual aspect is called time dilation. This states that a clock on an Earth-launched spaceship traveling at a very high velocity relative to an Earth observer who is stationary will move significantly slower than an identical clock in the observer's hand.

According to the time dilation prediction of relativity, if one twin traveled close to the speed of light in a spaceship and then returned to Earth, he would discover that he had aged very little compared to his aged (or perhaps long dead) twin who had remained on the Earth. Quite strange, isn't it? But Einstein's prediction of time dilation has been confirmed by experiments comparing highly precise atomic clocks in orbit around the Earth to atomic clocks on the ground. An additional prediction is that a clock will run slower in a gravitational field as compared to one that is not in a gravitational field. Again, this has been verified experimentally. In fact, the GPS location system that is now in widespread use must correct for these relativistic time effects in order to make accurate location measurements on the Earth, due to the fact that the GPS satellites are moving at orbital velocity relative to the Earth.

Another prediction of Einstein's theory is that a moving object's length will appear shorter to an observer who is not moving relative to that object. This is called Lorentz contraction. Such an observed change in length only becomes appreciable at speeds close to the speed of light. For example, at a speed of 95,000,000 miles per hour (approximately 14% of the speed of light), the length of an object would decrease by only 1% as observed by the observer. However, at 90% of light speed, the observed object length would be 50% shorter than its stationary length.

A further prediction is that the observed mass of an object will increase as observed by an observer who is relatively stationary. This means that as an object moves faster and faster, its mass becomes greater and greater and it takes increasing amounts of energy to get the object to increase its speed. Since relativity theory predicts that the mass of an object becomes infinite at the speed of light, this dictates that no object can ever be accelerated to the speed of light, since this would require infinite energy. Indeed, such effects have been observed in ultra-high-energy particle accelerators here on Earth.

Having briefly summarized the current scientific understanding of the theory of relativity and the very large (i.e. the cosmos), let's now proceed to discuss the scientific understanding of the very small. Quantum mechanics is the field of physics that deals with descriptions of the very tiny. It describes the behavior of sub-atomic particles, the electrons, protons, and neutrons that make up atoms, and the molecules made from atoms. It also describes the interactions of these species with electromagnetic radiation. Scientists consider quantum mechanics to be the basis for our understanding of how very small bits of matter and energy behave.

The roots of quantum mechanics go back to a concept put forward by Nobel Prize winner Max Planck in 1900 that electromagnetic radiation could be emitted by a heated body only with certain discrete energies that he termed "quanta". These discrete energies were the product of the frequency of the radiation multiplied by a term, h, which is now called "Planck's constant".

Quantum mechanics is based upon a famous equation called the Schrodinger wave equation. However Erwin Schrodinger, the scientist who formulated it, said that had he known to what use his equation would be put (namely as the basis for quantum mechanics), he would never have published it. Similarly, Einstein did not believe in quantum mechanics. His famous quote is that *"God does not play dice"*.

Why were Einstein and Schrodinger so adamantly opposed to quantum mechanics? Because it appears to strain scientific logic as we know it in all other aspects of science. The Nobel Prize winning "father" of quantum mechanics, Niels Bohr, famously said that anyone who wasn't disturbed by quantum mechanics didn't understand it. Here are some examples that illustrate this conceptual difficulty.

In quantum mechanics, matter can behave either as a particle or as a wave, depending on the conditions of observation. This is called particle-wave duality. Let's consider the electron. If you have electrons running down a metallic wire, they act like individual particles. This is the basis of electricity. However, if electrons pass through a finely-spaced grating, they act like waves, forming interference patterns. This is the basis of the electron microscopes that are used to greatly magnify objects. So which is it? In the most fundamental sense, are electrons particles or are they waves? What is their inherent nature? And why do they appear to behave differently based on the type of observation that is made.

The double-slit experiment was considered by Nobel Prize winning physicist Richard Feynman to be the best illustration of the particle-wave duality nature of quantum mechanics. The experiment is as follows. You have two fine parallel slits that electrons can pass through. On one side of these slits you have a source of electrons and on the other side a detection screen that tells you where an electron that passed through one of the two slits was located. Once an electron passes through a slit, it strikes the screen and leaves an image of where it struck. If the electron acts like a particle, then you will have only two slit-like images on the detection screen, since some of the electrons will pass through the left slit and some will pass through the right slit. That's what you would expect if the electrons behaved as only particles.

However, this is not what you observe experimentally. Experimentally, you see more than just two slit-like images on the screen. What you see is an array of multiple parallel lines, with the intensity of the lines decreasing as you move away from the central two lines. This pattern is called a diffraction pattern and is characteristic of waves that are passing through a double-slit configuration. So what does the double-slit experiment tell you? First it tells you that the electron was a particle when it struck the detection screen. Second it tells you that the electron seemed to be a wave when it actually passed through the double-slits. Confusing, isn't it?

It gets weirder. If you put detectors at each of the two slits so that you can directly observe which slit an individual electron passes through, then the experimentally observed pattern is that of just two slit lines, as would be the case if electrons were particles. So if you don't make an observation of which slit the electron actually passes through, you get a wave pattern on the detection screen. But if you make an observation of which slit the electron passed through, then you get a particle pattern on the detection screen. Such experiments have conclusively shown that the type of observation you make determines what kind of electron reality you will observe. Reality is determined by the act of observation!

This type of particle-wave duality is not only observed for electrons, but also for photons, which are considered to be the "particles" that make up visible light and all other electromagnetic radiation. Experiments have also shown that carbon particles formed from 60 carbon atoms configured in the shape of a soccer ball (termed Buckminster fullerenes in the scientific literature) also show the particle-wave duality behavior.

The Schrodinger equation is the fundamental equation of quantum mechanics, which is used to describe the location and energy of particle-wave duality entities. This equation is based on a variable written as Ψ. Quantum mechanical solutions to the Schrodinger equation all occur as Ψ^2, which is taken to be the probability that a particle will occupy a given region of space. So Ψ^2 is a probability. But what is Ψ? Quantum mechanicists will tell you that Ψ is a "possibility wave". But that's not a very satisfying explanation because a "possibility wave" has no physical meaning.

What the Schrodinger equation calculates is the probability that a particle will occupy a given region of space under the conditions that are specified at the start of the calculation. The Schrodinger equation constitutes the "mechanics" part of quantum mechanics. Quantum physicists plug in the experimental conditions, crank through the complex mathematics, and out pops a solution that can be observed by experiments. The major problem is that, until the act of observation is made, all the possible solutions of the Schrodinger equation are equally possible. The quantum mechanical terminology here is that the wave function calculated by the Schrodinger equation "collapses" to the observed solution as a result of the act of observation.

Erwin Schrodinger, the scientist who discovered the fundamental quantum mechanics equation that bears his name, put forward the following thought experiment to illustrate the difficulty that the act of observation plays in the reality described by quantum mechanics. It is called the "cat-in-the-box" experiment. A box contains a cat, along with a mechanical device that tracks the decay of a radioactive particle, which is a quantum event. If the radioactive particle decays, then the mechanical device releases a toxic gas that kills the cat. Now, before a person opens the box and takes a look (the act of observation), quantum mechanics says that the two states for the particle are equally possible, that is, the particle can decay or it does not decay. So then, logically, the cat is both dead and alive before the box is opened and the observation is made. That is the reality put forward by quantum mechanics.

Finally, consider quantum mechanical action-at-a-distance. Under certain conditions, two particles of light, two photons, can be emitted simultaneously from an atom, but traveling in opposite directions. Such photons are said to have quantum mechanical properties that are "entangled". Quantum mechanics predicts that by measuring a particular quantity of one of these so-called "entangled" photons, its polarization state, then the polarization state of the second photon is also determined. Effectively, the two photons are linked together even though they are physically separated. And it doesn't matter whether the two photons are separated by a fraction of an inch, one foot, 100 feet, 1 mile, 1000 miles, 1 million miles, or 100,000 light years when you make your measurement on the first photon. The properties of the other photon are also instantaneously determined, even if the other photon may be across the galaxy! The physics community calls this phenomenon "nonlocality".

The Irish physicist John Stewart Bell conceived of a way to experimentally measure photon entanglement and when the measurement was made in the 1980's, this prediction of quantum mechanics was actually observed to occur. The experimental verification of nonlocality as a real physical phenomenon has very profound implications. Einstein deridingly termed this *"spooky action at a distance"* and did not believe that it was possible because it takes place instantaneously (i.e. much, much, much faster than the speed of light) and does not involve the application of any physical forces that we know of. Yet, we now know that nonlocality is a phenomenon of nature.

So the three major mysterious aspects associated with quantum mechanics are: 1) particle-wave duality; 2) the role of the act of observation in creating reality; 3) nonlocality (spooky action at a distance). At the famous Solvay Conference in 1927, Albert Einstein and Erwin Schrodinger argued that the theoretical formalism of quantum mechanics was lacking in a foundation in physical reality. However, Niels Bohr and Werner Heisenberg won the day, and since that time quantum mechanics has been one of the two pillars of modern physics. The fact is that quantum phenomena are observed experimentally. Particle-wave duality is a reality of our universe. The act of observation dictating the outcome of a quantum mechanical experiment is a reality of our universe. Spooky action at a distance (nonlocality) is a reality of our universe. These phenomena have been experimentally observed and established. How can the reality of these phenomena be explained?

What is the physics interpretation of reality associated with quantum mechanics? The one accepted by most physicists is the Copenhagen interpretation put forward by Niels Bohr in the 1920's. This interpretation divides things into two realms, the macroscopic and the microscopic. The macroscopic realm is that of our everyday experience and also that of our scientific measuring instruments. In this realm classical physics applies. The microscopic realm is that of small things such as atoms and sub-atomic particles, where the Schrodinger equation describes the physics. The macroscopic instruments then make the observations that cause the wavefunctions of the microscopic world to coalesce into the observed state.

Basically, the Copenhagen interpretation says, as the famous quantum physicist John Wheeler put it, that *"no microscopic property is a property until it is an observed property"*. In other words, the microscopic world has no intrinsic reality. Only that which is observed is real. Kind of hard-to-swallow, isn't it? But that is the essence of the Copenhagen interpretation of quantum mechanics. Here is what Niels Bohr said:

"There is no quantum world. There is only an abstract quantum description. It is wrong to think that the task of physics is to find out how nature is. Physics concerns what we can say about nature."

The problem with the Copenhagen interpretation that observation creates microscopic reality is this: Who is the observer? Is the observer the piece of experimental equipment that makes the observation? The famous mathematician John von Neumann, in his 1932 comprehensive treatise on quantum mechanics "The Mathematical Foundations of Quantum Mechanics" (considered by many to be the "bible" of quantum mechanics), argued that no equipment could be the observer since any piece of experimental equipment can be considered as part of a larger quantum mechanical system. He observed that only a conscious observer could make the actual observation that collapsed the wavefunction to its observed value.

Another problem is that, while quantum phenomena clearly happen at very small scales of matter, when things get bigger the quantum nature disappears and things revert to the normal behavior that we see in our everyday lives. How the act of observation is associated with the transition from quantum scale effects to non-quantum classical effects is not at all clear. In other words, how does the larger environment act in some way as the observer?

Yes, the role of observation in creating the reality has given physicists major heartburn since the beginnings of quantum mechanics. In 1957, the physicist Hugh Everett put forward a concept called the "many worlds" interpretation that did away with the act of observation. The "many worlds" interpretation says that there is no observational collapse of the wavefunction. Instead, all the possible outcomes of the wavefunction occur in reality; it's just that each of them happens in a distinct, separate universe. So the act of observation is replaced by an infinite number of co-existing universes, the so-called "multiverse". Stated another way, there is no single reality but rather an infinite number of realities. Mindboggling, yet physicists are increasingly being attracted to the "many worlds" interpretation because of the difficulties associated with explaining how observation creates reality.

In summary, the quantum phenomena of particle-wave duality, the act of observation, and nonlocality are firmly established by experimental physics. These phenomena are inextricably interwoven into the fabric of our physical existence. However, according to quantum mechanics the reality that forms the basis of these phenomena either does not exist (Copenhagen interpretation) or consists of an infinite number co-existing universes ("many worlds" interpretation). At its root, quantum mechanics seems like a bizarre dream.

Everyone who is seriously involved in the pursuit of science becomes convinced that a spirit is manifest in the laws of the universe.

Albert Einstein

Fundamentals in Physics:

Let us take another step into the physics framework and consider what physicists call "fundamentals" of nature. These fundamentals are physical quantities that cannot be described as combinations of other physical quantities. Such fundamentals apply to all of the physical "stuff" in the universe.

Spacetime, Energy, and Charge are fundamentals of nature as conceived by our present science. All of these fundamentals came into existence at the event of the Big Bang which is thought to have taken place 13.8 billion years ago when "Everything" popped out in a single point from "Nothing".

Spacetime is the framework in which all the physical "stuff" in the universe exists. It is conceived as a continuum, meaning that it changes smoothly from point-to-point. Each point in spacetime is characterized by three dimensional coordinates and one time coordinate. Spacetime is the basis of Einstein's theory of relativity.

Energy is the next fundamental. Physics textbooks will tell you that the definition of energy is "the ability to do work". However, this is not a very satisfying definition because it states what energy does, but not what energy is. In fact, no one really knows what the essence of energy is. There are many different forms of energy such as kinetic energy, potential energy, heat energy, electrical energy, electromagnetic energy, nuclear energy, and also physical matter. For unknown reasons, it is a law of nature that energy is never created or destroyed when it changes form, it is always conserved.

Physical matter is just a form of "condensed energy". All matter has a quantity called "mass". What is mass? The most basic way to define it is as the "rest (or invariant) mass". The rest mass of matter, m, is related to the energy contained in the matter by Einstein's famous equation $E = mc^2$, where c is the speed of light in a pure vacuum. This relationship shows that mass and energy are fundamentally the same. In a nuclear bomb, a small amount of mass is converted into a tremendous amount of energy because the speed of light is such a large number. In a nuclear accelerator, the energy of two protons colliding can be converted into a very small additional mass of subatomic particles.

In his theory of general relativity, Einstein showed that the presence of large amounts of mass can warp the fabric of spacetime, thus producing the apparent force of gravity. Although all matter has mass, photons of electromagnetic radiation such as visible light have no mass. They are massless entities. Despite being massless, photons do possess energy through the famous Planck equation $E = h\nu$, where ν is the frequency of the photon radiation and h is a fundamental constant called Planck's constant.

Charge is another fundamental of nature. Charge is a property of matter that causes the matter to experience a force when in the presence of other pieces of matter that contain charge. Charge comes in elementary units that are given the symbol "e", and can be either positive or negative. Charged particles of the same sign repel each other, while charged particles of opposite signs attract one another. The charge on a proton in the nucleus of an atom is +1, while that of an electron in an atom is -1. Unlike matter, photons of radiation such as visible light have a zero charge.

So there you have a brief summary of the foundations on which our current physics rests. These form the basis of the present scientific explanation of physical reality. As you may have noticed, the fundamentals themselves are just "there" because they allow the current scientific theories to explain the results obtained from scientific experiments. However, they are themselves essentially metaphysical, because we can go no further in understanding the "why" of them with our present science.

Everything we call real is made of things that cannot be regarded as real.

Niels Bohr

Physical Makeup of the Universe:

Matter:

Our current physics says that the universe is made up of both the energy and matter that we can presently detect. All the stars, planets, asteroids, comets, dust, and atoms in the universe reside in a sea of energy. The universe is composed of matter and energy, and the forces that allow their interactions.

Physicists presently have what they call the Standard Model of matter. Start with a chuck of stuff, say a dinner spoon for example. The spoon is composed of individual atoms. There are a limited number of different types of atoms in our known universe, and each different atomic type is called a chemical element. Each individual atom is considered to be composed of a nucleus and surrounding orbital clouds of electrons. Because the nucleus is much smaller than the electron clouds, most of the atom is empty space, essentially a vacuum. Thus, all physical matter is mostly empty space!

The different atoms in our universe are represented by what is called the periodic table of the elements. This table was discovered in 1869 by the Russian chemist Dmitri Mendeleev based upon an ordering of the chemical properties of the different elements. The columns of the table contain elements that have similar chemical properties, and the sequence of the elements in the periodic table is dictated by the atomic number of the element, which is the number of protons in the nucleus of that particular type of atom. Thus, hydrogen is the first element in the periodic table, with an atomic number of 1 since it has only one proton. Among some of elements commonly known to the general public, carbon has an atomic number of 6, nitrogen is 7, oxygen is 8, aluminum is 13, iron is 26, copper is 29, silver is 47, gold is 79, and uranium is 92. It should be noted that elements of higher and higher atomic number continue to be discovered. The current highest element has an atomic number of 118, and is presently specified by the Latin pronunciation of this number, ununoctium. The periodic table is essentially the chemist's starting point for investigating chemical reactions, since it also provides an ordering of the chemical bonding electrons of the various elements, as dictated by the fundamental theory of quantum mechanics.

In addition to the atomic number, each element has what is called an atomic weight. The atomic weight is essentially the sum of the weights of the protons and neutrons that make up the atomic nucleus (the weight of the electron is only 1/1836 of the weight of a proton or neutron and is thus negligible in comparison). The weight of a single proton (or neutron) has been measured to be 1.673×10^{-27} kilogram. Because the individual atoms of an element can have a different number of neutrons in the nucleus (i.e. different isotopes), the atomic weight of the element is given as the average over all the possible isotopes of that element.

So atoms are made up of protons, neutrons, and electrons. Electrons are fundamental particles, but not protons and neutrons. These are composed of smaller particles which are called quarks. This rather strange name was put forward by Nobel Prize winner Murray Gell-Man who found this unusual word in the book "Finnegans Wake" by James Joyce. According to the Standard Theory, protons are composed of two up-quarks and one down-quark, while neutrons are composed of one up-quark and two down-quarks. Don't ask what up- and down- mean. Another fundamental property is charge. Protons have a charge of +1, neutrons have zero charge, and electrons have a charge of -1. These particles also possess a fundamental property called "spin". One should not regard the particles as actually spinning. Rather, the property of spin derives from the theory of quantum mechanics. Electrons, protons, and neutrons all have a spin value of ½ , for reasons that derive from quantum mechanics.

In addition to protons, neutrons, and electrons, there are other types of particles encountered in the Standard Theory. These include positrons (electrons with a charge of +1), anti-protons (protons with a change of -1), electron neutrinos (no charge and almost no mass), muons (a more heavy variant of the electron), muon neutrinos, tau particles (heavier than muons), and the tau neutrino (postulated but not yet discovered).

Positrons and anti-protons are termed anti-matter particles. Positrons and anti-protons have even been combined to synthesize anti-hydrogen atoms. While the amount of naturally-occurring anti-matter in our observable universe is almost vanishingly small, scientists surmise that there may be whole far-distant galaxies that are composed entirely of anti-matter. We should hope these hypothesized galaxies are very, very far away from us indeed, for whenever an anti-matter particle encounters a matter particle, they immediately annihilate each other in a flash of blinding energy.

Neutrinos constitute an important class of sub-atomic particles because of the fact that there are so many of them in the universe (they are generated by reactions in stars). Most of the neutrinos that strike the Earth emanate from our Sun as a result of the nuclear reactions that occur there. Because neutrinos have no charge and a very, very, very small mass (thought to be less than one millionth of the electron mass) they exhibit almost no interactions with ordinary matter. In actual fact, about 65 billion neutrinos per second hit every inch of your body all the time, but essentially pass right through it without affecting your body in any way.

All the particles we have described thus far are called matter-particles. But there is also another class of particles called force particles. In the Standard Model, these are the particles which transmit the four fundamental forces of nature. Photons are the force particles that transmit the electromagnetic force. Particles called gluons are the bearers of the strong nuclear force which holds the quarks together in protons and neutrons. So-called W and Z particles are the bearers of the weak nuclear force responsible for some forms of radioactivity. And gravitons are particles that are the bearers of the gravitational force. All of these force particles, except gravitons, have been experimentally discovered.

There is one more force particle that is postulated by the Standard Theory. This entity is called the Higgs particle and is thought to transmit the fundamental quantity of mass to all the other matter particles. In the popular media, the Higgs particle is referred to as the "God particle", based on Nobel Prize winner Leon Lederman's book by the same name. Lederman has admitted that his actual name for the particle was the "goddamn particle" because it was so important to the Standard Theory but so difficult to observe. Perhaps the name was shortened by his book editors, a circumstance that may have made it even more controversial. The Higgs particle has now been discovered by experiments at the Large Hadron Collider (LHC) in Geneva, Switzerland.

Electromagnetism:

We in the 21st century use electricity every day to make our lives easier and more productive. Electricity proves our light, heat, transportation, communications, and a whole other host of human activities. We are so familiar with the uses of electricity, but what do we really know about the phenomenon of electricity itself. Is electricity just physical in nature, or does it extend into the non-physical as well? This is the question that we will attempt to explore.

Electric Charge:

Any discussion of the topic "what is electricity" must begin with a discussion of what electric charge is, since electric charge is the fundamental quantity associated with electricity.

Electric charge is usually defined by physics as the following: Electric charge is the physical property of matter that causes it to experience a force when close to other electrically charged matter. You will notice the inadequacy of this definition. Physics considers electric charge to be a fundamental property and, as such, it cannot be further described. So at its root, physics has no explanation whatsoever as to what electric charge truly is, only what it does.

Electric charge is taken as either positive or negative. What makes it positive or negative, and what is the meaning of these terms? No scientist knows. Charge could just as easily be called yin and yang. Like charges repel each other while unlike charges attract. What is the reason for this? How would things be different if like charges attracted and unlike charges repelled?

The present scientifically-accepted unit of electric charge is the coulomb. The value of the coulomb is set as follows: 1 coulomb = the electric charge transported by 1 ampere of electrical current in 1 second. Now, the definition of an ampere is: 1 ampere = the transport of 1 coulomb of electric charge past a given point in 1 second. One can see from this definition of the electric charge as a coulomb that the definition is a circular one. It provides no insight whatsoever as to what electric charge is.

Another unit of electric charge is the statcoulomb. The statcoulomb is defined by the force equation that gives the force exerted by one electric charge on another electric charge that are separated by a distance: $F = q_1q_2/r^2$, where F = electric force, q_1 and q_2 are the two electric charges, and r = the distance between these two charges. The units of electric charge based on this force equation have the following units: charge in statcoulomb = $(\text{mass})^{1/2}$ $(\text{length})^{3/2}$ $(\text{time})^{-1}$. At least in this definition of electric charge, it is expressed in units of mass, length, and time, unlike the coulomb electric charge definition. Still, it tells us little as to what electric charge actually is because it is based on what electric charge does, namely produces a force between separated electric charges.

One thing we might consider doing to arrive at more insight into the nature of electrical charge is to incorporate Einstein's equivalency of energy and mass: $E = mc^2$. This means that the units of charge are: $(\text{energy})^{1/2}$ $(\text{length})^{1/2}$. It would indicate that charge has a relationship to energy. Is electric charge some sort of localized stationary wave pattern in its true nature? Physics has no evidence for this at present, but it might be considered as a possibility.

So the bottom line is that physics has no idea what electric charge actually is, only what it does. Electric charge is a fundamental property of physics. You might also call it presently metaphysical in nature.

Electron:

The particle-wave duality of quantum mechanics says that an electron is simultaneously a particle and a wave. Let us first discuss the particle aspects of the electron.

Physics says that the electron is an elementary particle. This means that it is not composed of an assembly of smaller particles. At least, physics has not yet found that the electron can be decomposed into smaller, constituent particles. Physics believes that all electrons are identical in their particulate makeup. Every electron in the universe is identical to every other electron in the universe.

An electron is a sub-atomic particle of matter. The electron is considered to be a highly stable particle, with a lifetime that exceeds 6.6×10^{28} years (this vastly exceeds the lifetime of the universe which is thought to be 13.8×10^{9} years, or 13.8 billion years old). It possesses the properties of mass, charge, and spin. The mass of an electron is approximately 9.109×10^{-31} kilograms which is exceedingly small. It is only 1/1836th the mass of a proton. The electron has an elementary electrical charge of -1.602×10^{-19} coulomb, where the coulomb is the unit of electric charge. An electron is said to have a "spin" of ½.

Mass is a property of the electron, so let us ask the question: What is mass? Mass is often defined in physics through the inertial equation $F = ma$, but this really states the effect of a force on a mass. Einstein showed that mass was equivalent to energy via the famous equation $E = mc^2$. Thus, mass is nothing more than "condensed energy". The energy equivalent of a single electron is 8.18×10^{-14} joule. The electron is a little bundle of energy.

What is the electric charge? That is a very good question indeed. Physics textbooks say that electric charge is the physical property of matter that causes it to experience a force when placed in an electric field. There are two types of electric charges: positive and negative. Like charges repel and unlike attract. The electron has the smallest amount of negative electric charge that a physical particle can have, while a proton has an equal amount of positive electric charge in relation to the electron's elementary negative charge.

So the electric charge is defined by the force it produces between two charged particles. And what is the nature of this electrical force? Current physics does not have any explanation, this force is essentially a "metaphysical something" that produces force across a physical distance. One might say that it is "spooky action at a distance". Only the characteristics of the electrical force produced by the electrical charge are known. The electrical force is proportional to the quantity of electric charges on the two separated particles, and inversely proportional to the square of the distance between the two particles. Whether the electrical force is attractive or repulsive depends on the sign of the particle electrical charges. Oppositely charged particles attract each other and same charged particles repel one another.

Now, what is electron "spin"? Normally, when you say something is spinning, you think of perhaps the spinning of a top. The top is rotating rapidly around an axis of revolution. Why are electrons considered to be "spinning"? It's because they appear to possess an intrinsic magnetic field that presumably results from the spinning of their electric charge. But physicists are quick to point out that it is not as simple as this. For example, to account for the magnitude of the observed magnetic field (also called the magnetic moment) of the electron, the electric charge of the electron would have to be moving faster than the speed of light! So what is electron spin? Actually, no one really knows.

What is the shape and size of the electron particle? Physics seems to agree that the shape of the electron is spherical. However, the size of the electron is another matter. The "classical" radius of the electron is given by physics as 2.8179×10^{-15} meters. By way of comparison, the size of a proton is about 0.84×10^{-15} meters, so the classical electron is more than a factor of three larger than the proton.

But there is much controversy in physics about the quantum mechanical "size" of an electron. Mathematically in quantum mechanics, it is treated as a "point particle" which has no size at all. However, other physicists say that this is physically impossible because the electron has a definite mass and if it were a point particle, then the electron would have an infinitely large density. Other quantum mechanicists say that you cannot even talk about a size for the electron, because the electron is nothing more than a probability density function in the Schrodinger wave equation. So the size of the electron is presently an open question in physics.

According to quantum mechanics, electrons exhibit behavior that is both particle-like as well as wave-like. Electrons exhibit particle-wave duality, as demonstrated by the famous double-slit experiment.

If an electron has a wave-like nature, then what is its wavelength and frequency? The so-called de Broglie wavelength of an electron is given by the equation: wavelength = h/mv, where h is Planck's constant, m is the electron mass, and v is the electron velocity. The value of Planck's constant h = 6.626×10^{-34} m^2 kg/sec. The electron's rest mass is 9.109×10^{-31} kilograms. Now we still need to select a velocity for the electron. Since electrons are never considered by physics to be absolutely at rest, let us use the typical velocity of electrons in an electric circuit for the wavelength calculation. The random speed of an electron in an electrically conducting metal such as copper is 1.57×10^6 meters per second. Using these values, the wavelength of an electron is 4.633×10^{-10} meters. By way of comparison the wavelength of visible red light is 7×10^{-7} meters. So the electron wavelength is much, much smaller than visible light. This is the reason why electron microscopes can image objects that are much smaller than can be seen using optical microscopes.

Since the velocity of a wave is given by the product of its wavelength and its frequency (velocity = wavelength x frequency), the frequency of an electron with a velocity of 1.57×10^6 meters per second is: frequency = 3.389×10^{15} Hz (cycles per second). By way of comparison, red visible light has a frequency of 4×10^{14} Hz.

The above provides a description of the electron as the physics of today understands it. One can see that there is much which is not understood about the nature of the electron. The least understood aspects are electron charge, electron spin, and whether the electron is a particle or a wave, or both simultaneously (particle-wave duality).

Electric Field:

An electric field is basically a convenient way to describe the electric force acting on an electric charge by a surrounding array of other electric charges that are separated by various distances from that electric charge. The definition of an electric field rests upon the force exerted on one charged particle by another charged particle: $F = q_1q_2/r^2$.

If we have an array of charges surrounding the test charge, the force on the test charge from the various charges in the array is simply the sum of the individual forces produced by these charges. Now, force is a vector quantity, which means that the force has both a magnitude and a direction. So each vector force must be added in order to get the magnitude of the force and the direction in which the force acts on the test particle.

In almost all situations, the details of the array of charges that surround a test charge is not known. For this reason, the sum of the forces produced by this array is taken to be the electric field at the test charge. Because it is a sum of forces, the electric field at a given point has both magnitude and direction, that is, the electric field is a vector quantity.

The electric field is given by the following equation: $E = F/q$. Here F is the vector sum of electric forces and q is the charge of the test charge. So the units of electric field are force/charge.

The electric field E described thus far is the static electric field. This means that the array of charges that produce the electric field do not change their relative positions or charge levels with time. Electric fields that do change with time are called electromagnetic fields.

Magnetic Field:

Magnetism is a word that has a degree of similarity with the word mysticism. Perhaps there is a reason for that.

Humans first discovered magnetism a long, long time ago. In fact, magnetism was discovered much before electricity was known to mankind. Magnetism was first noticed when people observed that the mineral lodestone had the property of attracting iron to it. Lodestone is composed of the mineral magnetite. The word magnet is a Greek word, since lodestones were found in the Greek location of Magnesia.

Lodestones were employed as primitive compasses for navigation by the Chinese in the 11th century. People discovered that a needle of lodestone showed a tendency to point in the north and south directions. This is how the "north" and "south" poles of magnets were first named.

The magnetism in lodestone arises from the magnetic moments of the electrons in the atoms that compose the lodestone. Physics says that each electron acts as a tiny bar magnet because of both its orbital motion around the nucleus of its atom, as well as its electron "spin". This is because the electron has an electric charge and when this electric charge moves, it produces a magnetic field. The atomic nucleus also possesses a magnetic moment, but it is very small in comparison to the electron magnetic field.

The magnetic field of the electron has a "north" pole and a "south" pole. But there are no individual "north" poles and "south" poles. The "north" pole has an associated "south" pole, and that is why magnetic moments are always dipolar in nature. Science has yet to discover the existence of a single, isolated magnetic monopole. So magnets always have a north-south pole configuration. The magnetic field is taken to begin at the "north" pole and end at the "south" pole.

Magnetic fields are similar to electric fields in the sense that these fields are both vector quantities, and they both produce a force at a distance. However, magnetic fields are fundamentally different from electric fields in that there are no magnetic monopoles (at least none have yet been discovered by science) whereas electric fields have electric charge monopoles. Magnetic fields only possess magnetic dipoles.

If you take a bar magnet with its "north" and "south" poles, and cut it in half, the two halves will then have their own "north" and "south" poles. You can cut a bar magnet into smaller and smaller pieces and this will always be true. If you cut so small that only an electron is left, that electron will still also be a magnetic dipole. Why is it that only magnetic dipoles are observed in nature? That is a very good question which physics has yet to answer.

Magnetic fields, like electric fields, are associated with action at a distance. However, unlike electric fields, it is now an array of magnetic dipoles that produces a magnetic force at a point in space. Another difference is that, while an electric field extends out to infinity from the point of its origin at an electric charge, magnetic fields always form closed loops around the "north" and "south" poles.

One thing a magnetic field will do is provide a force that tends to align other magnetic dipoles that are in the vicinity of the field. This characteristic is often employed to image the magnetic field around a bar magnet, by observing the alignment of iron filings that occurs as a result of the field forces.

Another aspect that a magnetic field does is to exert a force on an electric charge that is moving through the magnetic field. This force can cause the moving charge to be deflected in its motion, with the amount and direction of deflection dependent on the charge sign, the charge velocity, and the angle of the charge velocity vector with the magnetic field vector.

The force on an electric charge produced by a magnetic field is: F = (charge)(velocity)(magnetic field B)(sine of the angle between the velocity vector and the magnetic field vector). Thus, the units of the magnetic field B are (force)(time)/(charge)(length). This combination of units is referred to as a Tesla unit, named after the electrical genius Nikola Tesla.

Electromagnetic Induction:

A changing electric field produces a magnetic field, and a changing magnetic field produces an electric field. This is called electromagnetic induction. The field changes can be either changes due to time, or changes due to location. These phenomena were discovered by Michael Faraday in the 19th century. Faraday is also the person who coined the descriptive term "field".

A single moving electron produces a magnetic field in the plane perpendicular to it direction of motion, and this magnetic field is circular in shape around the axis of the electron's direction of motion.

Why does the single electron's motion produce this magnetic field? The answer to this is not known to physics. It is simply an experimental observation that it does so. The moving electron produces a surrounding magnetic field, but science does not know why this actually happens.

In a similar manner, changes in a magnetic field produce an electric field. In this case, we cannot look at a single moving magnetically-charged particle, since magnetic monopoles have never been experimentally observed to exist, although their existence is theoretically possible. There would be a very nice symmetry with electric charge if magnetic charges existed, but science has not found such magnetic charges to date. Given this fact, one employs changes in the magnetic field configurations with time or position that are said to induce the electric field.

Because of the experimentally observed fact that changing electric fields produce magnetic fields and changing magnetic fields produce electric fields, science considers electricity and magnetism to be intimately related, and thus these related field phenomena are termed the "electromagnetic field".

Maxwell's Electromagnetic Field Equations:

In the 19th century shortly after Faraday's discovery of electromagnetic induction, the Scottish physicist/mathematician James Clerk Maxwell developed an elegant series of equations that describe all the aspects of the electromagnetic field, including the induction aspects produced by field changes in position or time. It is fair to say that Maxwell's equations form the basis of the electrically-based technology that exists today.

Maxwell's equations have the following form:

Law	Equation	Physical Interpretation
Gauss's law for $\vec{\mathbf{E}}$	$\oiint_S \vec{\mathbf{E}} \cdot d\vec{\mathbf{A}} = \frac{Q}{\varepsilon_0}$	Electric flux through a closed surface is proportional to the charge enclosed
Faraday's law	$\oint \vec{\mathbf{E}} \cdot d\vec{\mathbf{s}} = -\frac{d\Phi_B}{dt}$	Changing magnetic flux is associated with an electric field
Gauss's law for $\vec{\mathbf{B}}$	$\oiint_S \vec{\mathbf{B}} \cdot d\vec{\mathbf{A}} = 0$	The total magnetic flux through a closed surface is zero
Ampere – Maxwell law	$\oint \vec{\mathbf{B}} \cdot d\vec{\mathbf{s}} = \mu_0 I + \mu_0 \varepsilon_0 \frac{d\Phi_E}{dt}$	Electric current and changing electric flux is associated with a magnetic field

I will not go into the mathematics of these equations in detail here, but just briefly indicate what each of them describes. The first equation (Gauss's law for E) says that the electric field flux leaving a surface is proportional to the charge contained inside that surface. This basically says that the intensity of an electric field depends on the quantity of electric charge that produces the electric field. The second equation (Faraday's law) says that the electromotive force (i.e. voltage) induced in a closed electrical circuit is proportional to the rate of change of the magnetic flux that the circuit encloses. It is a description of the magnetic field induction of an electric field. The third equation (Gauss's law for B) says that the total magnetic field flux passing through a closed surface is zero. This equation basically results from the experimental fact that magnetic monopoles have not been observed to exist. Because of this fact, magnetic fields must always form closed loops. The fourth equation (Ampere-Maxwell law) states that the magnetic field induced around a closed circuit loop is proportional to the electric current plus displacement current (rate of change of electric field) that the loop encloses. This describes the electric field induction of a magnetic field.

Electromagnetic Radiation:

characterized by describing near-field and far-field conditions in the vicinity of the antenna.
In the near-field, the electromagnetic fields are still "attached" to the conditions of the antenna, namely the moving electrical charges in the antenna. However, at a certain distance from the antenna, the fields break free from the antenna charges and then become moving electromagnetic waves, termed far-field waves. The details as to how this break-away of the moving far-field waves occurs from the non-moving near-field conditions are currently not well understood by science.

Hertz showed that electromagnetic waves can be formed in an open-ended range of frequencies and wavelengths. For electromagnetic waves, the frequency and the wavelength are related to each other through the equation: speed of light = (wave frequency) x (wave wavelength). The range of electromagnetic waves currently observed by science ranges from long waves having wavelengths of many kilometers, to gamma rays with very, very small wavelengths.

Photon:

The story of the photon begins with the German physicist Max Planck. In 1900, Planck was attempting to explain the frequency and temperature dependence of the radiation that was emitted from a so-called "black body" radiator (a "black body" is a material that absorbs all radiation that impinges upon it, hence the reason for calling it black). When you heat such a material it begins to emit invisible radiation in the infrared, then upon further heating it becomes visibly red, then with higher temperature it changes to orange, and finally at the highest temperatures it appears white hot. It is this behavior that Planck sought to explain.

In order to develop an equation describing the intensity of the emitted radiation as a function of temperature and radiation frequency, Planck could only do so if he assumed that the radiation was being emitted in the form of individualized quanta, or little packets of electromagnetic wave energy. Each little quantum packet of energy was taken to have an energy given by $E = h\nu$, where h is termed Planck's constant and ν is the frequency of the electromagnetic radiation.

The energy of each little quantum is very, very small and so Planck's constant is also a very, very small number. Planck's constant = 6.626 $\times 10^{-34}$ joule-second (units of energy x time are termed "action" in physics).

In the year 1905, Albert Einstein published a paper on the photoelectric effect. The photoelectric effect is the observation that light impinging on the surface of a material can eject electrons from that material.

A central observation of the photoelectric effect is that the frequency of the light must be above a certain threshold frequency in order to have any electrons ejected, regardless of the intensity of the radiation that is below the threshold frequency.

In order to explain the photoelectric effect, Einstein in 1905 proposed that the light impinging on the material surface was in the form of "light quanta", or individualized little packets of light energy, rather than the continuous electromagnetic waves described by Maxwell. In this theory, Maxwell's continuous light waves were actually composed of vast quantities of individualized "light quanta particles", each individual quanta particle being a discrete, far-field electromagnetic wave packet. Interestingly, it was not until the year 1926 that the word "photon" was coined for these "light quanta particles" by Gilbert Lewis. Physics now considers not only light but all electromagnetic radiation to be composed of individualized photons.

The individual photon is conceived as having no mass and no charge. As an electromagnetic wave, the photon travels at the speed of light. It can do this and still conform to Einstein's theory of relativity because the photon is taken to have no mass.

Although a photon has no mass, physics says that it does possess a momentum. Since momentum is defined as (mass) x (velocity), how is this possible? This results from the two equations $E = mc^2$, the equivalency that Einstein showed between energy and mass, and the equation proposed for the energy of the photon $E = h\nu$ by Max Planck. By combining these two equations, one obtains a "virtual mass" of the photon equal to $h\nu/c^2$. Since the photon always travels at the speed of light c, then the photon momentum = $h\nu/c$.

It seems physically counterintuitive that the photon has no mass but possesses a momentum. Yet experiments have shown that beams of photons can produce a physical pressure on material that does possess mass. This is the reason that "solar sails" in space can produce some thrust to propel a space vehicle.

Because photons have no mass and no charge, they cannot interact with each other. So the light photons, microwave photons, and radio/television photons that float around together in our technological society do not interfere with each other. They are effectively invisible to each other.

Photons do possess a "spin" which is also called a polarization. This polarization is taken to the direction of the rotation of the photon's electric and magnetic fields around the axis that defines the direction of its travel. This polarization can have two values, left rotation and right rotation. Photon polarization is the reason that the polarized lenses in sun glasses can filter out some of the photons that travel through them.

Is the photon a wave or a particle? Just as with electrons, current physics says that it is both. Experiments with single photons have verified this particle-wave duality. How do you generate a single photon that you can run such an experiment on? This is how.

A single atom, molecule, quantum dot, or defect center is isolated and then stimulated to a higher energy configuration with a pulsed radiation source. When the excited species decays down to its ground state, the emission of a single photon occurs. This single photon can then be employed for further experimentation.

Single photons have been employed in particle-wave duality experiments. In such experiments, beam splitters are used to direct the single photon along different paths. A beam splitter is an optical device that allows half of an incident beam of photons to pass through the beam splitter and the other half to be reflected from the beam splitter.

Now when a single photon encounters a beam splitter, it can either be transmitted through the splitter or reflected from the splitter, but it will not be divided into two particles so that it goes both ways. Experiments with single photons have clearly shown that a single photon will go one way or the other, but not both ways. This observation supports the particle aspect of the photon.

However, if an additional beam splitter and two reflecting mirrors are added to the experiment to allow the two possible photon paths at the first beam splitter to recombine, one observes wave-like interference effects for both of the photon paths. This observation supports the wave aspect of the photon.

One may ask the question, how can the wave-like nature of the single photon be split in two at the first beam splitter? Physicists have no physically-based rationale for this wave splitting. It is currently a metaphysical mystery of particle-wave duality.

So the photon is a little, individualized packet of electromagnetic radiation, and single photons can be produced for experimentation. One can then put forward the following logical question: What is the size and shape of a single photon?

This is a question that is really quite difficult for our current physics to answer. The detailed structure of the photon is not well understood. In a general sense, the size of the photon can be approximately taken as the photon wavelength. The wavelength of 3 kilohertz radio waves is 100 kilometers. The wavelength of the 2.45 gigahertz microwaves in your microwave oven is 12.2 centimeters. And the wavelength of the visible light spectrum is 400-700 nanometers.

One practical application of photon size occurs in your microwave oven. The front of your microwave oven has a metal screen with small holes in it that allows you to see what is inside the microwave when it is heating. You can do this because the wavelength of visible light is small in comparison to the holes in the screen, so light photons can easily pass through the holes. However, the diameter of the holes is much smaller than the wavelength of the microwaves, so the microwaves cannot pass through the metal screen to the environment outside of the microwave cavity. If microwaves were able to do so, anyone standing near the door of a microwave oven would receive a detrimental microwave radiation exposure.

The exact shape of the photon is also very little known. One would think that the shape would be related to the magnitude of the oscillating far-field electric and magnetic fields that make up the photon. But there is very little experimental data about photon shape. In 2015, a group of physicists were able, for the very first time, to construct an image of a single photon confined to the length of a very small silver nanowire, showing its undulating electric and magnetic fields.

What is it like to be a photon?

In order to answer this question, we must discuss Einstein's special theory of relativity. How did Einstein come to develop this theory? He said that when he was 16 years only, he had the thought: What would it be like to ride on a beam of light? He thought that if he could do so, then he would be able to directly observe the electric and magnetic fields that Maxwell said make up the light beam (it seems remarkable that a 16 year old boy would know the work of Maxwell, but then again, he was Einstein).

In the year 1905, Einstein published his special theory of relativity. He was seeking to explain how the speed of light could be constant in all relative frames of reference moving at a constant speed, given the experimental observation of this in the Michelson-Morley experiment of 1887. Einstein said that the constancy of the speed of light was a fundamental principle of physics, and then proceeded to show what the ramifications of this constancy of light speed would be for the reality of space and time.

In order to make the speed of light constant in all reference frames, it was necessary to modify how both space and time are interpreted in terms of reality. Specifically, space and time were no longer independent of each other (as Newton assumed), but rather were intimately melded together in a new quantity called spacetime. Only with this change in physical paradigm could the constancy of the speed of light be explained. Essentially, the quantities of space (i.e. location) and time are intermixed in the coordinates that define each frame of reference when the speed of light is taken as an invariant quantity.

The ramifications of Einstein's special theory of relativity were truly mind-blowing. Here are the most important ones. First, the times measured in two different reference planes that are moving relative to one another are not the same. From the perspective of a person in a "stationary" reference plane, the time that is being measured by another person in a reference plane that is moving with respect to the first person is slower than the time measured by the person in the "stationary" plane. Basically, this is saying that the measurement of time is relative and determined by the relative speed of the timepiece. Now, you might say how can you tell who is the stationary person and who is the moving person. The answer provided by physics is that the moving person is the one who has accelerated away from the stationary person.

That the measurement of time is not a constant at all points in the Universe is deeply counter-intuitive, but is actually true. Experimental measurements of extremely accurate atomic clocks that are moving relative to each other have shown that they will not record the same time, but different times depending on the relative speeds of the clocks. As an example, the space-based Global Positioning System depends on satellites that are moving in orbit around the Earth at high speeds relative to the surface of the Earth. In order to provide accurate locational measurements of locations on Earth, the GPS must apply relativistic corrections to its measurements of time, otherwise the calculated positions will in inaccurate. A "stationary" clock will move faster than a clock that is moving with respect to the "stationary" clock. This effect is call time-dilation.

Another ramification of Einstein's special theory of relativity is that lengths measured by observers in different frames of reference will not be the same. If, for example, a "stationary" observer is looking at an object that is traveling rapidly with respect to him, he will see that object as being a little shorter in length than it actually is in its own frame of reference. This is called length-contraction. An additional feature of special relativity is that anything that has mass will increase in mass with increasing velocity.

The above special relativity effects, namely time dilation, length contraction, and mass increase, will only be observed to a large extent when the speed something is traveling at begins to approach close to the speed of light c. At the speeds that we on Earth normally travel, none of these effects can be observed by us because they are so vanishing small (except the GPS time dilation effects, but these are only observed because atomic clocks with extreme accuracy are available to us).

Now we can come back to our question: What is it like to be a photon? A photon has no charge and no mass, and travels at the speed of light. What does this mean in terms of Einstein's special theory of relativity? Well, first it means that the photon does not experience time at all - any clock moving at the speed of light will never tick. The photon exists in a state of no-time. A further consequence is that, although we perceive in our frame of reference that the photon travels at light speed, from the photon's perspective it does not travel at all, it never moves. From the photon's perspective, it is "born" and "dies" at the same spot in spacetime.

So the photon sees of itself that it has no charge, no mass, experiences no time, and is stationary in the spacetime continuum. That is what it is like to be a photon. The photon appears to be something that exists in another reality altogether!

Range of Photons:

The electromagnetic photon spectrum is open-ended on both the low frequency and high frequency ends. What are the limits for the lowest frequency (largest wavelength) and highest frequency (smallest wavelength) photons currently known by science? Let us describe these limits.

The lowest end of the man-made electromagnetic spectrum is termed Extremely Low Frequency (ELF). ELF frequencies are in the range of 3 to 30 Hz (cycles per second). These ELF photons have wavelengths in the range of 1,000,000 to 100,000 meters, respectively. Such frequencies are able to penetrate long distances within the earth and through seawater, and so are used for communications in deep mines as well as with submarines. However, their use is limited by the size of the antenna transmitters and receivers required which must be a significant fraction of the ELF wavelength.

What is the lowest possible frequency and largest possible wavelength for a photon in the physical realm? One could say that such a photon would have a wavelength the size of the observable universe. And what is the size of the observable universe? Our current science says that the diameter of the observable universe is approximately 93,000,000,000 light years across. This is equivalent to 8.8×10^{26} meters. Now you might ask yourself, how can the diameter of the observable universe be 93 billion light years, since the age of the universe is only thought to be 13.8 billion years. The reason for this difference is that space itself has been expanding since it is postulated by science to have first come into existence in the Big Bang 13.8 billion years ago.

If we assume a photon with a wavelength of 8.8×10^{26} meters and since the speed of light is approximately 3×10^{8} meters/second, then the frequency of the lowest possible frequency photon would be 3.4×10^{-19} Hz. So here we have the lower frequency photon limit for a photon that could exist in the observable universe.

Now let us turn our attention to the highest frequency photons. The highest frequency photons here on Planet Earth are the gamma rays produced by the radioactive decay processes of atomic nuclei. A common source of gamma rays is the radioisotope cobalt-60. Cobalt-60 emits a gamma ray of energy 2.13×10^{-13} joules. Using the Planck equation $E = h\nu$, this corresponds to a frequency of 3.21×10^{20} Hz and associated wavelength 9.35×10^{-13} meters. Cobalt-60 gamma rays are highly ionizing radiations that are lethal to living organisms. This radioisotope is employed medically to kill cancer cells, and used to irradiation foods in order to kill off unhealthy microorganisms.

The highest energy gamma rays observed to date come from cosmic sources outside of Earth. These cosmic gamma rays have frequencies in the range of 10^{25} to 10^{28} Hz and associated wavelengths in the range of 10^{-17} and 10^{-20} meters, respectively. The astronomical processes that produce these very-high-frequency gamma rays are not adequately understood by science at the present time.

How are these very-high-frequency photons detected? They are detected indirectly via a cascade process. When the very-high-frequency gamma rays from space first encounter the upper reaches of Earth's atmosphere, they strike an atomic nucleus located there, which leads to the formation of an electron-positron particle pair. The electron-positron pair almost immediately reacts to form a slew of secondary gamma rays of lower frequencies due to reactions with other nuclei, which eventually leads to the formation of so-called Cerenkov light radiation that can be detected with optical detectors. So the detection of very-high-frequency gamma rays is done through the indirect detection of the cascade of particles and lower-frequency gamma rays that they produce.

One can now ask the question: What are the highest frequency photons that could be possible in our universe?

The smallest length that our science can presently conceive of is the so-called Planck length. The Planck length is an exceedingly small length indeed. A Planck length is 1.6×10^{-35} meter, which is approximately 0.00000000000000000001 the size of a proton. To put this into conceptual perspective, if a dot one-tenth of a millimeter in size (which is about the smallest size dot that the human eye can distinguish) were magnified to the size of the observable universe, then a Planck length would be a dot one-tenth of a millimeter in size! That's how small a Planck length is.

An electromagnetic wave that would have the Planck length as its wavelength would have a frequency of 1.88×10^{43} Hz. Such a frequency is 10,000,000,000,000,000 larger than the highest frequency cosmic gamma rays that have been detected by science to date, and the energy of these Planck length waves would also be

10,000,000,000,000,000 times greater than the highest frequency cosmic gamma rays.

Changing the Frequency of Photons:

Science says that photons in free travel do not interact with each other in any way because they have no charge and no mass. Two photons traveling toward each other from opposite directions in a head-on collision will pass through each other without interacting, and will be unchanged after the passage. Actually, this seems strange, since each photon is composed of electric and magnetic fields which one would think could add or subtract to each other when the two photons were in contact superposition, but experimental results to date have shown that there are no such effects.

Can photons change their frequency? The Planck equation says that the frequency of a photon $\nu = E/h$, so the frequency of a photon can be changed by changing its energy. If a photon's energy is reduced, its frequency will be reduced. If a photon's energy is increased, the photon's frequency will increase.

How can a photon change its energy? A photon can interact with the electrons in atoms, being absorbed by the atom such that electrons in the atom change their energy level to a higher level. When the electron drops back to its equilibrium energy level, it then emits a photon. The emitted photon is usually of lower energy than the absorbed photon.

However, there is one situation where photons can increase their frequency and that is called "frequency doubling". Frequency doubling was first demonstrated by researchers in 1961. The demonstration was made possible by the invention of the laser, which created the required high intensity coherent light. The researchers focused a ruby laser with a wavelength of 694 nm into a quartz sample. Then they sent the output light through a spectrometer, recording the spectrum on photographic paper, which indicated the production of light at 347 nm. Frequency doubling occurs when light enters some types of crystals because of non-linear atomic polarization.

Einstein's theory of relativity says that gravity can change the frequency of a photon. A photon that is generated in a field of lower gravitational potential will be reduced in its frequency (i.e. be red-shifted) when it encounters a field of higher gravitational potential. Similarly, a photon that is generated in a higher gravitational field will increase its frequency (i.e. be blue-shifted) when it moves into a region of lower gravitational field. The reason for these gravitational photon frequency shifts is due to gravitational time dilation effects.

While the frequency of individual photons can only be influenced by their energy or by their gravity environment, the frequencies of streams of photons can be modulated in order to transmit informational signals. This is the basis of the frequency modulation (FM) of radio waves. In the FM transmission of radio waves, an electrical signal corresponding to the sound information is imposed upon the transmitter of the carrier radio waves, such that the frequency of the radio waves produced is related to the sound electrical signal. Thus, the stream of radio wave photons varies in frequency with time. At the receiver station, this FM modulated radio wave stream is converted back to a sound electrical signal through the use of demodulator electric circuits.

In principle, it should be possible to frequency modulate beams of any type of electromagnetic radiation to transmit information. However, the technology to do so is presently difficult for microwaves, light waves, and higher frequency electromagnetic radiation.

Zero-Point Energy Field:

Max Planck was the first to propose the existence of zero-point energy, which he did in 1912. He hypothesized that the radiation from blackbody radiators must have a ground state energy equal to $h\nu/2$ at the temperature of absolute zero. The zero-point energy concept was incorporated into quantum mechanics by Heisenberg and the Heisenberg uncertainty principle, which states that no physical quantity can have both a known momentum and known location at the same time. One or the other must be uncertain, even at absolute zero temperature. Hence, even at absolute zero, the particles/waves must be "jiggling" with an energy = $h\nu/2$.

In 1916, Walther Nernst speculated that the universe is filled with zero-point energy. The zero-point energy is referred to as the "vacuum energy". What this means is that a complete vacuum containing no matter particles will still have an energy associated with it. One can think of this zero-point vacuum energy as composed of photons with all possible values of photon frequencies. Since the photon energy depends on the photon frequency ($E = h\nu$), the higher frequency photons will contribute more to the zero-point energy than the lower frequency photons.

The best experimental evidence that zero-point energy exists is the Casimir effect. The Casimir effect was discovered in 1948 by Hendrik Casimir. If you have two conductive metal plates that are positioned very close to one another with nothing in between and with no electric fields or magnetic fields present, the two plates will experience an attractive force. The reason for this attractive force is said to be that zero-point photons with wavelengths longer than the spacing between the plates are excluded from this region, and because of this exclusion the zero-point photons exert a compressive force on the plates. The Casimir effect has been experimentally verified many times and can become an important influence in things like extremely small electronic components.

Not only is the universe stranger than we imagine, it is stranger than we can imagine.

Arthur Eddington

Some Key Questions within Physics:

To my mind, there are a number of questions concerning the underpinnings and constitution of our present understanding in physics. Let me attempt to point out some of these.

Origin of the Universe:

How did the universe come to be? The currently-accepted physical theory is that the universe began approximately 13.8 billion years ago in a "Big Bang". Actually, the name Big Bang was a derogatory term coined by the famous astronomer Fred Hoyle, who espoused the opposing theory that the universe has always existed. It's interesting to note that the person who first formulated the Big Bang theory was a Belgium Catholic priest by the name of Father Georges Lemaitre. Lemaitre put forward the essence of the Big Bang theory in 1927, based on Einstein's general theory of relativity. The famous astronomer Edwin Hubble discovered experimentally that the distant galaxies in the sky were moving away from us, indicating that the universe was expanding. The discovery of the cosmic microwave background is also key to the foundations of the Big Bang theory, since this is thought to be the afterglow of that original stupendous event.

At the very first infinitesimal fraction of a second of the Big Bang, spacetime, energy, matter, and all the laws of physics came into being. Everything instantaneously appeared from "Nothing"

There are two key questions about the Big Bang that scientists struggle with. The first is: What caused the Big Bang? And the second question is: Where was everything before the Big Bang happened? Some theorists have suggested that the Big Bang was produced by the point source collision of multi-dimensional "membranes". The unfortunate thing about such theories is that they are impossible to prove or disprove by scientific experimentation, which puts them in the class of metaphysics rather than physics. As Terence McKenna nicely put it:

"Modern science is based on the principle: "Give us one free miracle and we'll explain the rest". The one free miracle is the appearance of all the mass and energy in the universe and all the laws that govern it in a single instant from nothing."

One needs to ask the question: Was there really a Big Bang in the first place? Is it possible that the universe is much, much older than 13.8 billion years? Could it be that the universe exhibits periodic eras of expansion and contraction that occur over time scales of billions of years. In other words, the universe "breaths". Right now, we are living in the period of universe expansion, and that is why we observe that space appears to be expanding. Is the cosmic microwave background really the afterglow of a Big Bang explosion, or is it due to something else altogether?

The major experimental elements supportive of the Big Bang are the Hubble expansion of galaxies and the cosmic microwave background. Let us consider each one of these elements.

The Hubble expansion of galaxies is based upon the observed red shift of light that is detected. For example, the characteristic emission lines of hydrogen in distant galaxies are shifted to longer wavelengths (i.e. red shifted) and this red shift is taken to be the result of the fact that these galaxies are moving away from our vantage point here on Earth. This motion is considered to be related to the expansion of space itself that is occurring as a result of the Big Bang, because all of the far away galaxies appear to be moving away from us, with the velocity of this relative motion increasing with distance between us and the far away galaxy. This is called Hubble's law after astronomer Edwin Hubble who first experimentally determined it. The value of the Hubble's law constant is 67.15 ± 1.2 (km/s)/megaparsec. A parsec is an astronomical unit of distance. One parsec equals 3.26 light-years.

Now Hubble's law depends on two things, first the amount of red shift observed say in the spectral lines of hydrogen, and second the distance away from us that the galaxy producing the red shifted light is located. It may be that the red shift is not related to a velocity shift effect at all, but is due to some other mechanism, such as photon interactions with interstellar gas clouds or perhaps even "Dark Matter". And with regard to cosmological distances, these are measured using what are termed "standard candles". Standard candles are astronomical objects that are presumed to have known, constant luminosity independent of their distance from the Earth. The question is: How standard are the standard candles? It seems to me that this is an open question at the moment.

The cosmic microwave background is considered to be the thermal "afterglow" of the Big Bang event. However, another possibility is that it merely represents the background radiation that emanates from the collection of stars in the universe. It does not necessarily need to be the remnant afterglow of a Big Bang.

Cosmic Inflation:

In an infinitesimal fraction of the first second of time following the Big Bang, the universe is postulated to have "inflated" at a rate vastly exceeding the speed of light to a size level not too dissimilar from the present postulated size of the universe. The inflationary period lasted from 10^{-36} second after the conjectured Big Bang singularity to sometime about 10^{-32} second after the singularity. During this infinitesimally small amount of time, the universe was said to expand by a factor of at least 10^{26}. In order to do so, this inflation expansion had to exceed the speed of light, thus violating the theory of relativity. However, the somewhat hand waving rationale for dealing with this issue is that spacetime can move faster than the speed of light as long as no information is transmitted between those elements that are moving faster than light.

Inflation theory was first developed in 1979 and it attempts to explain the origin of the large-scale structure of the cosmos on the basis that quantum fluctuations in the microscopic inflationary region, magnified to cosmic size, became the seeds for the growth of structure in the universe.

This rather bizarre theory was postulated in order to account for the uniformity of the universe that we observe in all observational directions today, both the relatively uniform arrangement of galaxies as well as the uniformity of the cosmic microwave background. Yet, what caused "inflation" to happen (if it indeed did), the mechanism by which it happened, and how it was possible for "inflation" to exceed the speed of light are clearly open questions in physics.

Expansion of Space:

The observable universe is taken to be a roughly spherical region encompassing all matter that can be observed from Earth at the present time, because electromagnetic radiation from these objects has had time to reach Earth since the beginning of the cosmological expansion. There are at least 2 trillion galaxies in the observable universe, containing more stars than all the grains of sand on planet Earth. Assuming the universe is isotropic, the distance to the edge of the observable universe is roughly the same in every direction (assuming of course that the Earth is located not too far away from the center of the sphere).

How large is the universe? If the Big Bang happened 13.8 billion years ago, then one might expect that the universe is a sphere with a radius of 13.8 billion light-years, right? Actually not. Based on the Hubble constant, space itself has been expanding at a rate of 67.15 kilometers per second per megaparsec. So taking this space expansion into account, the radius of the universe is actually 46.5 billion light-years. The diameter of the universe is thus 93 billion light-years, a phenomenally large number.

This size is termed the cosmic event horizon. We cannot observe anything that is outside of this horizon because the light from such events will never be able to reach us.

So the size of our observable universe is a sphere with a diameter of 93 billion light-years. But what is outside of our observable universe? In other words, what is our universe expanding into? This is a question presently unknown to science. Some scientists think that the actual universe is much larger than our observable universe alone because inflation at the start of the Big Bang caused it to become very, very large, essentially infinite from our perspective. On this basis, what our observable universe is expanding into is a moot point, because it is essentially similar to what our observable universe is composed of, namely a relatively uniform array of galaxies and galaxy clusters in all directions.

Other scientists may say that our observable universe is essentially expanding into “nothing”, because “nothing” can exist in the absence of spacetime. This begs a definition of the meaning of “nothing”.

Not all the galaxies are moving away from us, however. The galaxies that are relatively close to us, our local galaxy group, are actually moving toward us due to the attraction of gravity. For example, the Andromeda galaxy, which is 2.5 million light-years away from us at the present time, will eventually collide with our Milky Way galaxy in about 4 billion years. So, locally, the force of gravity is overcoming the expansion of space.

If space is expanding, are the things that are in space also expanding? This is a good question. Are the galaxies, stars, planets, even you and I also actually expanding as space itself expands? Some scientists say yes and some say no on this point. Those who say yes state that the things in space also expand, but at an essentially unobservable rate because the distances involved in them are so small, as well as because any measurement “rulers” will also be expanding. Those who say no argue that the forces of gravity and electromagnetism act to hold things together against the space expansion.

What about Dark Energy? Dark Energy is taken to be an intrinsic property of empty space. So if space is expanding, then the amount of Dark Energy must also increase with this expansion. This sounds like the creation of energy from “nothing” and seems to violate the physical law of conservation of energy. This is a puzzle indeed.

And finally, what is causing the expansion of space? Scientists currently say that it is the repulsive force of Dark Energy that is responsible. What is Dark Energy and why does it produce a repulsive force? These are presently questions unanswered by science.

Composition of the Universe:

The current cosmological Standard Theory says that only 5% of the universe is composed of the matter and energy that we can presently detect! 25% of the universe is "Dark Matter" and the remaining 70% is "Dark Energy". An analogy for this is what a person sees when he (or she) looks at a sparsely populated mountainous region at night. You can see the pinpoints of light from the residences of the people who live there, but you cannot see the mountains. Why are these things called "Dark"? Because our current science cannot explain them. They are dark to our understanding.

Dark Matter, what is that? No one knows at present, but scientists say that we are all swimming in it. Dark Matter passes through your body all the time, but does not interact with the normal matter (i.e. matter composed of protons, neutrons, and electrons) that make up the atoms of your body. Science says that Dark Matter exists because of the gravitational effects that it has on ordinary matter. Our galaxy, the Milky Way, is encased in a sphere of Dark Matter. And so are all the other galaxies in the universe.

But it has been very difficult for scientists to detect any semblance of Dark Matter. One prime candidate has been weakly interacting massive particles (WIMPs). However, exquisitely sensitive experiments conducted in highly sheltered environments such as deep mines in the Earth have failed to detect any evidence of WIMPs thus far. After decades of searching and experimentation, physicists still have no clue as to the nature of Dark Matter. In fact, there are some scientists who argue that Dark Matter does not really exist at all. Rather, they say that the astronomical gravitational effects attributed to Dark Matter are actually reflections of the fact that the gravitational laws of physics are somehow dependent on the size scale upon which they act. Essentially they say that gravity is different for the "small scales" we experience in the solar system, as compared to the galactic scale or multi-galactic scale. So there is some scientific uncertainty as to whether Dark Matter is real or not.

Dark Energy is another unknown quantity altogether. Cosmologists describe the effects of Dark Energy as follows. If you have two volumes of space that are completely empty of matter, then these two volumes of empty space will repel each other, for reasons that are totally inexplicable at the present time. Essentially, these two volumes of space will exert a negative gravitational effect on each other. Science says that Dark Energy exists because there is no other way to explain the observational fact that the universe is continuing to accelerate in its expansion. The amount of Dark Energy in the universe is related to the size of the universe. As the universe expands in size, more Dark Energy is created. But created from where?

Universe Constants:

In his book entitled “Just Six Numbers”, astrophysicist Martin Rees described the six fundamental numbers that determine the characteristics of the universe. If these numbers were just a little bit different, human beings and indeed life itself, would not exist. The question is why these numbers are so finely tuned.

The first number is the number of spatial dimensions in the physical universe, D. The universe is a three-dimensional one and thus the value of D is equal to 3. Our physical experience is one of left-right, up-down, and forward-back. However, if D were 2, we would be living in the world of Flatland, and things would be drastically different. Similarly, if D were 4 our universe would contain an extra spatial dimension - call it “in-out” - and things would be vastly more interesting and complex than they are in our three-dimensional existence. Why does D equal 3 in our universe?

We now know that the galaxies that compose our universe are grouped into clusters and superclusters. The structuring is a result of forces and energies that were operative shortly after the Big Bang. This cosmic structure is characterized by a number, Q, which is the ratio of two fundamental energies, and has a value of about 1/100,000, a quite small number. Q can be thought of as an index of the smoothness of the expanding sphere of the cosmos. If the value of Q were smaller than 1/100,000, the universe would have few large-scale galactic structures. If it were larger, there would be a violent interaction of galactic clusters and superclusters, and the formation of immense black holes.

Will our universe, which supposedly began with a Big Bang, end by dissipation through endless expansion or will it eventually contract in a Big Crunch? The answer to this question depends on the cosmic number **Ω**. This number is the ratio of all the material present in the universe to a critical value of material that guarantees that gravity will ultimately attract all things back to a Big Crunch. When **Ω** = 1, the expansion energy of the universe exactly matches the gravitational contraction energy. For unknown reasons, the value of **Ω** was "tuned" to equal 1 in the earliest eras of the universe after the Big Bang. If **Ω** had been less than 1, stars and galaxies would never have had enough time to form by gravitational attraction. And if **Ω** had been greater than 1, the universe would have experienced a Big Crunch long ago. Either way, we would not be here now. At the present time, the value of **Ω** is estimated to be 0.3 (including both visible matter and Dark Matter), and it thus appears that the universe will continue expanding.

The next number is the so-called cosmological constant **λ**. Einstein was the first to propose the existence of **λ**, as a way to generate a static universe from his general theory of relativity. While Einstein's motive for **λ** has long been discounted since we are clearly living in an expanding universe, its value has taken on a new interpretation because of the discovery of Dark Energy. Dark Energy is a force of presently unknown character that acts as a repulsive force between the elements of space itself. It is Dark Energy that is causing the universe to continue to accelerate in its expansion and it is the action of Dark Energy that causes **λ** to have a very small but finite value. If **λ** had a value larger than its current one, the universe would have expanded too fast for stars and galaxies to have formed at all.

The processes that go on in our Sun are summarized in the number **ε.** **ε** reflects the amount of mass that is converted to energy by the nuclear fusion reactions that power the Sun. The observed value of **ε** is 0.007.

If this value were a little smaller, say 0.006, then the Sun would have a shorter lifetime but, more importantly, the Sun would not be able to produce the elements in the periodic table, of which our physical bodies are composed. Conversely, if **ε** had a value of 0.008, the Sun and the other stars in the universe would burn hydrogen so efficiently that there would be no hydrogen left over to form an essential ingredient for life, water. So if the number **ε** were only slightly different from its observed value of 0.007, life as we know it would not be possible.

The sixth number is N. This number measures the strength of electrical forces between atoms divided by their gravitational attractive force. The value of N is extremely large, equal to 1,000,000,000,000,000,000,000,000,000,000,000,000 (or 10^{36} in scientific notation). If N had a slightly smaller value, say 99.9% of its observed value, only a much smaller and much more short-lived universe could exist. The creatures in such a universe could be no bigger than apple seeds, and the time required for biological evolution would be short, thus significantly constraining the development of advanced species.

These six numbers essentially constitute a "recipe" for our universe. The question is: Why did this particular recipe lead to the existence of human beings? Some scientists say that we exist because that's just the way things are here in this physical reality. We are here because the universe is the way it is. Other scientists surmise that there may be an infinite number of other universes with different recipes, where life as we know it may or may not exist. Either approach begs the question as to why these six numbers are the way they are.

Existence of an Aether:

In the 19th century, the existence of an aether was a foundation of physics. Astronomers conceived that the sun and the planets traveled through it and that it was the medium which propagated the force of gravity. James Clerk Maxwell thought of it as the medium through which electromagnetic waves propagated. This aether was conceived as filling all of space, being of a universally stationary nature, and having physical properties such as the permeability and permittivity of free space.

However, as a result of the null result of the Michelson-Morley experiment in 1887, the existence of the aether was downgraded by the scientific community. Following the introduction by Einstein of his special and general theories of relativity, space was considered by many scientists to be simply empty of all physical phenomena, and hence no aether existed. It is worthwhile noting, however, the even Einstein did not completely rule out the existence of a modified type of aether. Here is his quote from 1920:

"We may say that according to the general theory of relativity space is endowed with physical qualities; in this sense, therefore, there exists an Aether. According to the general theory of relativity space without Aether is unthinkable; for in such space there not only would be no propagation of light, but also no possibility of existence for standards of space and time (measuring-rods and clocks), nor therefore any space-time intervals in the physical sense. But this Aether may not be thought of as endowed with the quality characteristic of ponderable media, as consisting of parts which may be tracked through time. The idea of motion may not be applied to it."

The theory of quantum mechanics clearly indicates that an aether environment is the site of the zero point field and energy that exists in a pure vacuum of space. Quantum mechanics says that there is definitely a great deal of energy in the vacuum, but the form of this energy is presently considered to be "virtual" in nature, whatever that may mean.

Dark Energy is another quantity likely associated with an aether. This is because the amount of Dark Energy increases as the amount of space increases in the expansion of the universe. So clearly, dark energy seems a characteristic of the vacuum aether.

At the present time, science appears to consider that the vacuum of space does indeed contain some aether-like substance. But the nature of this "new aether" is presently unknown.

Flow of Time:

Time is something that is central to our physical experience of reality. We observe a sequence of events happening in time, where a past event is the cause of a future event. We experience a flow of time, from past through present to future. And this flow has an arrow, an arrow of time. Time flows in only one direction, from the past to the future. We cannot alter the past and we cannot predict the future. We live in the present, the now, but the now is constantly changing. This is how we experience time in our daily life.

However, neither the theory of relativity nor the theory of quantum mechanics has any requirement for the linear, one-way flow of time.

Let us consider what the theory of relativity says about the flow of time. Essentially, it says that there is not flow of time at all. The universe is composed of "blocks" of stationary spacetime that exist. This is called the block universe. All times that are past, present, and future from our limited perspective exist in a kind of eternal Now. This is admittedly quite difficult for the average person to accept, but this is precisely what the theory of relativity says about the nature of time. The theory says that all aspects of time, past, present, and future are locked into an eternal Now of spacetime. Past and future are all there, forever.

If there is no flow of time, what about our everyday observations of cause and effect. We observe that a past cause produces a future effect. Indeed, this is the basis for experimentation in science. But in fact the theory of relativity makes no distinction between past and future. The theory works just the same in either direction of time. This is known as time-reversal symmetry. It means that things can occur either forward or backward in time. Cream added to coffee can mix, as well as unmix. An egg can break as well as un-break. There are no restrictions on this in the theory.

Now let us consider the flow of time as it applies in the theory of quantum mechanics. The basic equation of quantum mechanics is the Schrodinger equation. The Schrodinger equation dictates the probability of a particle existing at a particular place and time. The fact is that the Schrodinger equation exhibits time-reversal symmetry, so that the solution for time = t is the same as the solution for time = -t. Hence, quantum mechanics does not support the concept of a one-way time flow.

So neither the theory of relativity nor the theory of quantum mechanics incorporates a rule that there must be a one-way flow of time. Yet, our everyday experience says the opposite. How can this be? Some scientists say that the reason for this difference lies in the second law of thermodynamics. The second law deals with entropy, or the degree of disorder of a system. The second law of thermodynamics says that the entropy of a closed system always increases with time. Thus, this increase establishes a flow of time, and the fact that entropy always increases establishes an arrow of time. The problem with this explanation is that it only applies to large collections of individual particle interactions, and not to single particle interactions.

So where does the arrow of time stand in our concepts of physical reality? That is a very good question indeed. Why is it that the overarching theories of our current physics do not correspond with our everyday sense of time? There must be a reason for this.

Simultaneity in Relativity:

The theory of relativity is based upon the assumption that the speed of light is constant for all observers in all frames of reference. It is this assumption that leads to the melding of space and time into the quantity of spacetime. Thus far, all experimental tests of this assumption have verified it.

A consequence of the speed of light being constant in all frames of reference is that the existence of simultaneous events is rare indeed. According to the theory of relativity, only events occurring in frames of reference that are not moving relative to each other can truly be considered to be simultaneous (i.e. events occurring at the same "time"). This is because time itself is dependent on the relative motion of these reference frames. When the reference frames are moving at drastically different speeds or when they are located at great distances from each other, events will not appear simultaneous to observers in the two different frames.

Here is an example of this from the book "The Fabric of the Cosmos" by Brian Greene:

"To make this concrete, imagine that Chewie is on a planet in a galaxy far, far away— 10 billion light-years from earth— idly sitting in his living room. Imagine further that you (sitting still, reading these words) and Chewie are not moving relative to each other (for simplicity, ignore the motion of the planets, the expansion of the universe, gravitational effects, and so on). Since you are at rest relative to each other, you and Chewie agree fully on issues of space and time: you would slice up spacetime in an identical manner, and so your now-lists would coincide exactly. After a little while, Chewie stands up and goes for a walk— a gentle, relaxing amble— in a direction that turns out to be directly away from you.

This change in Chewie's state of motion means that his conception of now, his slicing up of spacetime, will rotate slightly. This tiny angular change has no noticeable effect in Chewie's vicinity: the difference between his new now and that of anyone still sitting in his living room is minuscule. But over the enormous distance of 10 billion light years, this tiny shift in Chewie's notion of now is amplified. His now and your now, which were one and the same while he was sitting still, jump apart because of his modest motion.

If Chewie walks away from you at about 10 miles per hour (Chewie has quite a stride) the events on earth that belong on his new now-list are events that happened about 150 years ago, according to you! According to his conception of now— a conception that is every bit as valid as yours and that up until a moment ago agreed fully with yours— you have not yet been born. If he moved toward you at the same speed, the angular shift would be opposite, so that his now would coincide with what you would call 150 years in the future! Now, according to his now, you may no longer be a part of this world."

Needless to say, the effects of relativity on simultaneity of events deviate drastically from our everyday, common sense notion of things happening at the same time. In fact, this strikes at the very heart of what we call linear time. There is no absolute time reference point anywhere in the universe.

What does this say about the reality of past and future events? It appears that both past and future are both definitely established quantities that exist concurrently with each other in the overall reality.

Reality in Quantum Mechanics:

The reality of quantum mechanics possesses a dream-like quality. Electrons and photons can behave as both particles and waves, and which type is seen depends on the characteristics of the observation that is made. The reality that is observed requires the presence of an observer, and the observer of choice is a conscious observer.

The Schrodinger equation describes the probability of an electron existing in essentially all locations in space, even those that are far from the eventually observed location of the electron. Before the electron is observed, it potentially exists in any or all possible locations. So before observation, where is the electron? It is essentially spread out over "probability space". Does the Schrodinger equation possess any elements of reality, or is it simply a mathematical tool used to calculate the probabilities of quantum mechanical outcomes?

Before the electron is observed, it essentially has no physical reality. As Niels Bohr said, the only reality is observed reality. This led Einstein to comment in derision that the moon does not really exist unless we are looking at it. Is there a reality independent of our observation of it? When a tree falls in the forest and there is no one to observe it, did it actually fall? Is there a reality distinct from the observational aspect.

And what of the nature of the observer? The famous scientist John von Neumann concluded that the observer must be a conscious observer in order to collapse the wave function to the level of reality that is actually observed in a quantum mechanical experiment. And what if there is no observer at all? In that case, how do quantum events collapse to yield the macroscopic reality that we all observe? Is there some way that the macroscopic environment present near a quantum event induces the collapse of the wave function?

Then we have the experimentally verified phenomenon of quantum non-locality, the spooky faster-than-light interaction between two entangled quantum particles. There is absolutely no understanding about how this non-local, instantaneous interaction takes place. It should be impossible in terms of the theory of relativity, since that theory says that nothing can move faster than the speed of light. Yet, experiments continue to confirm that non-local phenomena exist in our three-dimensional reality.

Zero-Point Energy:

Quantum mechanics says that there is a vast field of energy that permeates the entire universe. This field of energy apparently exists outside of our normal space and time. It is a seething configuration of electromagnetic energy of all wavelengths, from the very large to the smallest possible wavelength. The energy in the zero-point field would be infinite, were it not that scientists consider the shortest possible wavelength to be the Planck length.

Photons from this zero-point sea of energy are considered by current science to "pop" in and out of our three dimensional reality through a unspecified mechanism. They are referred to as "virtual" particles. They do not reside most of the time in our physical universe, but can appear and then almost instantaneously disappear back into the zero-point sea.

A major problem for science at the moment is the magnitude of the zero-point energy. Quantum mechanical calculations for the zero-point energy density yield values of the order of 10^{110} joules per cubic meter of vacuum. This is an extremely high energy density compared to all other observed energy density values in nature. The zero-point energy density would go to infinity if there were not a cutoff made for extremely high photon frequencies and energies associated with the smallest conceived physical length, the Planck length.

So, quantum mechanics yields an extremely high value for the zero-point energy density. On the other hand, the second major scientific paradigm, general relativity associated with cosmology, produces a very low value of the zero-point energy density. Recent measurements of the relative brightness of type Ia supernovae against their distance (inferred from the amount of the red shift of their light spectrum, as well as the light spectrum of other objects within the same galaxy) indicate that the universe is undergoing an accelerated rate of expansion, and not slowing down, as it was thought previously. This expansion is being attributed to a certain small vacuum energy density that has been given the term Dark Energy by cosmologists. However, the value of the zero-point vacuum energy density calculated from the cosmological measurements is extremely small, of the order of 10^{-9} joules per cubic meter of vacuum.

A difference of 10^{120} in the values of the zero-point energy density predicted by quantum mechanics compared to those predicted by general relativity is a major embarrassment and source of mystery in science at the present time. Nobel Prize winner Frank Wilczek has characterized the situation as follows:

"We do not understand the disparity. In my opinion, it is the biggest and most profound gap in our current understanding of the physical world. ... [The solution to the problem] might require inventing entirely new ideas, and abandoning old ones we thought to be well-established. ... Since vacuum energy density is central to both fundamental physics and cosmology, and yet poorly understood, experimental research into its nature must be regarded as a top priority for physical science."

If the quantum mechanics description of the vacuum zero-point energy density is correct, does the zero-point energy represent essentially a limitless source of energy that might be tapped from any location in the universe? There are a small number of physicists who think this might be possible, but none have been able to demonstrate the generation of "free" energy from the vacuum thus far. One can only say that the possibility of doing so may exist perhaps sometime in the future.

Laws of Physics:

Where do the "Laws of Physics" come from? The current paradigm of physics is that they appeared magically from nowhere at the instant of the Big Bang. There are so many Laws of Physics that physicists presume have existed in an unchanged manner since the Big Bang.

Here are some of the major "Laws of Physics": Conservation of Energy, Conservation of Mass, Conservation of Momentum, Laws of Thermodynamics, Newton's Laws of Motion, Maxwell's Equations, Laws of Relativity, Laws of Quantum Mechanics.

One must ask the question: How did all these Laws come into existence at the moment of the Big Bang. And a further question is: Why do these Laws have the form that they do?

Let us consider one particular Law of current physics, namely that the speed of light is constant in all frames of reference. This is the basis for Einstein's theory of relativity. It is under this assumption that the quantities of space and time are folded together into the new quantity of spacetime.

The speed of light is presently taken to have the value of 299,792,458 meters per second. This speed of light value is taken to be a constant of nature that has never changed since the Big Bang and that always remains at the same constant value.

However, the enlightened scientist Rupert Sheldrake had the audacity to question whether or not the speed of light is actually a constant or that perhaps it has changed, and is changing, with time. By going back into old speed of light measurement records, Sheldrake discovered that the measured speed of light had actually decreased in the time period of 1928 to 1945 by about 20 kilometers per second. After that it increased to its present measured value.

Sheldrake discussed this discrepancy with the Head of Metrology (metrology is the science of the measurement of constants) at the UK National Physical Laboratory. Here is the exchange that they had about this, from his book "Science Set Free":

"Sheldrake: What do you make of this drop in the speed of light between 1928 and 1945?
Metrologist: Oh dear you've uncovered the most embarrassing episode in the history of our science.
Sheldrake: Well could the speed of light have actually dropped? That would have amazing implications if so.
Metrologist: No, no, of course it couldn't have actually dropped. It's a constant!
Sheldrake: Oh well then how do you explain everyone was finding it going much slower for that period? Is it because they were fudging their results to get what they thought other people would be getting and the whole thing was just produced in the minds of physicists?
Metrologist: We don't like to use the word fudge.
Sheldrake: Well what do you prefer?
Metrologist: Well, we prefer to call it intellectual phase-locking.
Sheldrake: Well if it was going on then how can I be so sure it's not going on today and that the present value isn't produced by intellectual phase locking?
Metrologist: Oh we know that's not the case.
Sheldrake: How do we know?
Metrologist: Well. We've solved the problem.
Sheldrake: Well how?
Metrologist: Well we fixed the speed of light by definition in 1972.
Sheldrake: But it might still change.
Metrologist: Yes, but we'd never know it because we've defined the meter in terms of the speed of light. So the units would change with it."

In actual fact, the meter has been formally internationally defined as being the length traveled by light in 1/299792458 of a second. Given this definition of the meter unit of measurement by the current measured value of the speed of light, it now becomes virtually impossible for the science community to measure a value different from the current value. Thus, if the speed of light actually does change as the Earth propagates through different configurations of the universe, we humans will never know it! Totally absurd.

Some scientists have recently proposed that the speed of light may have been much greater than its present value at the time of the Big

Bang. This idea is presented as an alternative to the concept of inflation to explain the apparent uniformity of the universe that is observed in all directions.

Black Hole Singularity:

Einstein's theory predicts that light will be observably bent when it travels in the vicinity of massive objects in space. As was previously mentioned, this was first verified experimentally by Eddington in 1919. However, a further ramification is that Einstein's theory predicts the existence of "black holes". Black holes are objects in space where spacetime is so distorted (i.e. gravitational effects are so large) that nothing, not even light itself, can escape from them if it gets too close. Hence the reason why they are called "black". Black holes are postulated to form when large stars explode.

Scientists now have a body of astronomical evidence that black holes do indeed exist. In fact, there is thought to be a massive black hole at the center of our own Milky Way galaxy. The reason for this conjecture is because the stars at the galactic center move in very unusual high curvature orbits around an object that cannot be detected with our telescopes This object clearly has a massive gravitational field but it cannot be seen because it is dark and not emitting any electromagnetic radiation. Black holes are the true monsters of the universe. They are quite literally star and planet-eaters. Should a black hole come into the vicinity of our star and solar system, that would be the end of our local astronomical neighborhood and us in it.

Another reality aspect of black holes is the fact that at their center they are postulated to contain a "singularity", a mathematical point where spacetime and the laws of physics as we currently know them are changed radically.

The holy grail of current physics the Theory of Everything (TOE for short). At the present time there are two parallel theories that are intrinsically incompatible with each other. The first is general relativity which describes the very large bodies in the cosmos and their interactions through the action of gravity. The second is quantum mechanics that describes the observed behavior of very small things like atoms and sub-atomic particles. In almost all cases of the application of quantum mechanics to the material world, the force of gravity is neglected because it is so small in comparison to the electromagnetic force, and the strong and weak nuclear forces. But there is one area in the universe where this is not the case. That location is at the center of a black hole.

General relativity predicts that there is a singularity at the center of a black hole, a very small point-like region where gravity is so strong, the mass density is so high, and the fabric of spacetime is so warped that the theory of general relativity breaks down. Physicists absolutely detest singularities. So there must be some melding of general relativity and quantum mechanics that occurs at the center of a black hole. The two theories must be made to fit together there in order to have a Theory of Everything. But, try as they might, theoretical physicists have been unable to come up with any approach that can meld general relativity and quantum mechanics together.

The general nature of the incompatibility between general relativity and quantum mechanics is that general relativity is based on the concept of a continuum structure of spacetime, while quantum mechanics is based upon the existence of individual, non-continuum quantum entities.
In trying to come up with a Theory of Everything, scientists speculate that at the black hole singularity, spacetime itself becomes "granular", and that this granularity can then somehow be folded into a quantum mechanical description. But at the present moment, it is by no means clear how this might be accomplished within a theoretical framework.

Physics at the Planck Length:

The Planck length is the smallest possible length dimension thought to be able to exist in our three-dimensional physical reality. This length was originally suggested by Max Planck as a fundamental unit of length that could be defined using only major physical constants. The Planck length is given by the formula $L_p = (hG/c^3)^{1/2}$ and has a value of 1.616×10^{-35} meter, which is approximately 0.0000000000000000001 the size of a proton. Here, h = Planck's constant, G = gravitational constant, and c = speed of light in a vacuum.

Why did Planck put forward a length dimension that was so very, very small? The reason is that he wished to obtain a length that was only associated with fundamental physical constants relevant to physical theories. The constant h is fundamental to quantum mechanics, while the constants G and c are fundamental to general relativity. Based on dimensional analysis, the only way a length dimension could be obtained from these three constants was the form of the Planck length.

The Planck length is a vanishingly small quantity. By way of comparison, the smallest length that current science has been able to measure is of the order of 10^{-19} meter. So the Planck length is 16 orders of magnitude smaller than what science can presently measure.

Below the Planck length, the Laws of Physics as we know them do not apply. Electromagnetic waves are not defined quantities below the Planck length and neither are any quantum mechanical species. Some scientists say that spacetime becomes "granular" or "foamy" at the Planck length, whatever that might mean. Notions of space and time are considered to become physically meaningless at the Planck length. Interestingly, the Planck length is taken as the dimensional range of the "strings" that are associated with string theory. However since no one has ever measured a string, string theory remains only an unverified theoretical framework.

But why should there be a lower limit to the length dimension. Is it possible that some form of reality exists at and below the Planck length? Perhaps there are other dimensions of reality below this level.

All matter originates and exists only by virtue of a force... We must assume behind this force the existence of a conscious and intelligent Mind. This Mind is the matrix of all matter.

Max Planck

Non-Physical Phenomena:

Extrasensory perception (ESP) is the ability to perceive or perform certain activities in an apparently non-physical way. The term extrasensory perception encompasses phenomena such as clairvoyance (being able to "see" things that it is not possible for the eyes to physically see), telekinesis (being able to move or affect objects using only the mind), telepathy (mind-to-mind communication), and precognition (the ability to predict future events).

In his book "The Conscious Universe", Dean Radin summarized many of the scientific studies that have been performed to determine if ESP phenomena are real effects or not. The type of analysis employed is called meta-analysis, where the units of the overall statistical evaluation are independent ESP investigations that have been performed by a large number of different investigators. Hundreds of studies conducted with considerable scientific rigor were evaluated. Radin's meta-analysis results convincingly showed that clairvoyance, telepathy, and telekinesis are real effects that produce statistically significant results above those predicted by chance. All of the studies in the meta-analyses were of the double-blind type (i.e. the correct answer was not known by either the investigators or the subjects involved in the experiments).

Investigations of telepathy typically involve a "sender" attempting to send a mental image of a viewed image to a "receiver". In many investigations, when telepathic receivers were isolated by heavy-duty electromagnetic and magnetic shielding (specially constructed rooms with steel and copper walls) or by extreme distance, they were still able to obtain information from the sender. The most interesting telepathy studies are those that employ the so-called "ganzfeld" technique. Here, a person is placed into a condition of sensory isolation; they are lying down in a silent, soundproof room and their eyes are covered. The purpose of the sensory isolation is to increase the likelihood of detecting faint mental perceptions that might otherwise be obscured by normal sensory inputs.

In the case of clairvoyance, the situation is similar except there is no person who is a "sender"; rather, the "receiver" attempts to mentally "view" an image that has been concealed from his sight. The image may be in the same room as the "receiver", say inside a sealed opaque envelope, or it may be in a sealed envelope that is physically located at a different location completely, or the target may be a physical location that is remote from the "viewer".

Telekinesis studies typically involve attempting to use a person's will to influence the roll of a dice or the result of a binary random number generator that randomly generates either "1"s or "0"s. The random number generator experiments are particularly compelling since they do not involve a physical object such as a dice but rather just a computer generated number.

Meta-analysis studies have shown that in the case of clairvoyance and telepathy, correct "hits" are obtained approximately 60% of the time (as compared to a 50% chance hit rate) and for telekinesis 51% of the time (as compared to a 50% chance hit rate).While these percentages may seem relatively small to you, because of the large size of the statistical samples, the odds of their happening by chance alone are extremely low, of the order of 1,000,000,000,000 to 1. Such results clearly demonstrate that these ESP phenomena are real phenomena and not something metaphysical. It should be noted that even the highly skeptical scientist Carl Sagan thought the ganzfeld telepathy results and the random number generator psychokinesis results deserved to be seriously considered.

While quite definitive in terms of scientifically establishing the reality of ESP phenomena, these statistical analyses are somewhat dry in character and do not provide much insight into the characteristics of the phenomena that are being exhibited. One can get a much better feel for these phenomena through more detailed descriptions of some of the more startling ESP cases. We will now do this for the cases of clairvoyance and telekinesis.

Clairvoyance is a French word which translates as "clear vision". Perhaps the most interesting clairvoyance phenomena are associated with the remote viewing programs that were conducted in both the United States and the former Soviet Union.

In the early 1970's, clairvoyance experiments being conducted in the USSR prompted the U.S. government to establish experiments on remote viewing that might be used for obtaining sensitive and important information on potential enemy activities.

In the fall of 1972, a remote viewing program was begun under the aegis of the CIA at Stanford Research Institute in California by two laser physicists, Dr. Hal Puthoff and Dr. Russell Targ. The first remote viewer in this program was a New York artist and psychic by the name of Ingo Swann. Ingo Swann displayed a very high level of remote viewing capabilities, and was a key member of the initial remote viewing team. The code name for these CIA remote viewing activities was Project Stargate.

Ingo Swann might be described as a rather colorful person. This starts with his name, Ingo Swann, which was his real name. You just don't find that many people who have a first name of Ingo, and his full name Ingo Swann definitely suggests something exotic. Then there is the location of his birth, Telluride, Colorado where he was born in 1933 (he died in 2013). I don't know how many of you have been to Telluride, but it is one of the most scenic mountain locations in all of Colorado (along with its sister town Ouray, which is right across the mountain from Telluride). Telluride is a mountain resort area now but in 1933, at the height of the Great Depression, it was a very small mining town with a population of only 150.

Ingo had a relatively normal and apparently happy childhood. He was something of an introvert and also a voracious book reader. And he was very intelligent and curious about the nature of things. He graduated from college with a B.A. degree in 1955 and after that enlisted in the Army rather than being drafted. He spent most of his three-year Army tour in Korea and the Far East and upon leaving the Army settled in New York City with the goal of becoming an artist and painter. However, he quickly discovered that there were many "starving artists" in Gotham and so, to put bread on the table, he worked at the United Nations for twelve years. After that, he went back to painting and was able to at least subsist on the sale of his works.

While in New York, he made social contacts with people who were interested in paranormal phenomena and this eventually led him to become a test subject for the American Society for Psychical Research (ASPR). His initial experimentation was targeted at attempting to alter the temperature reading of an isolated and sealed thermistor, a device for precisely measuring temperature, by using only his mind. In these experiments, he achieved some success, enough for a publication in the Journal of the American Society for Psychical Research. This also brought him to the attention of the CIA. As Ingo said in his "Autobiographical Memoir":

"A confirmed example of controlled psychokinetic effects had been demonstrated by a subject in a laboratory. If he can trigger a thermistor could he not also trigger a nuclear bomb?"

At the ASPR, Ingo began experiments in 1971 with what was termed "remote viewing". It should be noted that in these experiments, Swann was more than just a guinea pig with psychic abilities. He actively participated in the design, conduct, and interpretation of the results and was instrumental in the development of a methodology for remote viewing.

The initial remote viewing methodology was quite simple. A number of sealed envelopes were created, each one containing the name of a U.S. city as well as the phone number of the weather service in that city. One of the sealed envelopes was selected by an ASPR person, who did not know its contents in advance. Then the name of the city was communicated to Ingo who was sitting in a chair with his head wired up to an EEG machine. Here is how Ingo Swann described the first successful remote viewing experiment in his memoir:

"Thus, after the morning and afternoon OOB practice sessions on December 8, 1971, and while I was still hooked up to the brainwave contraption, another ASPR worker, Vera Feldman, then handed Janet Mitchell a sealed envelope.

Through the intercom Janet said (I remember her words very clearly): "Ingo, I've got the envelope. Let me know when you're ready."

"I'm ready," I replied, even though I was also quite nervous.

So through the intercom I could her Janet tearing open the envelope. Then she breathed hard and said: "The target is Tucson, Arizona."

Now something wondrous and magical occurred.

Of course I really had no idea how to "get" to Tucson from the rather ugly experimental room in New York. And when I first heard the mention of "Tucson, Arizona," a picture of hot desert flashed through my mind.

But then I had the sense of moving, a sense that lasted but a fraction of a second. Some part of my head or brain or perceptions blacked out -- and THERE I was -- THERE. Zip, Bang, Pop -- and there I was... something I would refer to years ahead as "immediate transfer of perceptions."

So fast was the whole of this, or so it seemed to me, that I began speaking almost as soon as Janet had narrated the distant site through the intercom.

"Am over a wet highway, buildings nearby and in the distance. The wind is blowing. It's cold. And it is raining hard."

I didn't even have time to sketch this, for it was easy enough to articulate into the tape recorder.

Having said as much, I noted that there was water glistening on the highway -- and then said: "That's it! Tucson's having a fucking big rainstorm," although the forbidden word was not entered into the record of the experiment.

"That's it?" questioned Janet through the intercom.
"Yeah, that's it -- only that I'm slightly dizzy. I thought this would take longer. It's raining and very cold there."

"Okay," Janet replied, again breathing hard. Through the intercom I heard her dialing the number of the weather service in Tucson.

I was sweating, and started to pull off the electrodes. I noticed that my spine was tingling -- if that's the correct word.

Before I could stand up, though, Janet said through the intercom: "Well, you're right on, baby. Right now Tucson is having unexpected thunderstorms and the temperature is near freezing?"

I remember all of this with extreme clarity, largely because it was my first consciously experienced Zap-Pop biolocation thing. It is indelibly etched somewhere in "my mind."
It wasn't until I got home that evening that I realized while "at" Tucson I had completely lost perceptual and sensory contact with the experimental room at the ASPR -- even with my own body.

And I had no idea at all that this simple small thing would eventually lead into a very big thing, indeed -- and into circumstances which were so unusual that they bewildered very many."

That is how Ingo Swann described the beginning of the phenomenon of remote viewing. Now the story moves to the Stanford Research Institute in California.

Following Ingo's first remote viewing experience at ASPR, he began having difficulties with that organization. Perhaps the foremost difficulty was that the organization's journal declined to publish any of the remote viewing results that had been generated.

In March 1972, Swann had occasion to read a document written by Dr. Harold E. Puthoff, a laser physicist working at the Stanford Research Institute in Menlo Park, California. SRI was a government-supported organization with links to the Defense Department and the CIA. This document was a proposal to do some research in the area of quantum biology. Swann was so impressed with the content of Puthoff's document that he sat down and wrote Puthoff a letter saying that he was interested in investigating the boundary between the animate and the inanimate. Ingo also described some of the research results that had been obtained by him at ASPR.

When Puthoff received Swann's letter, he was intrigued by the results Swann had achieved in the ASPR work and was impressed enough to invite Swann to visit SRI for a week in June 1972 so that he could test Swann's psychic abilities.

Puthoff decided to put Swann's abilities to the test by having him attempt to influence the behavior of a very-well-shielded (physically, electrically, and magnetically), superconducting Josephson junction magnetometer that was being employed in a cutting-edge research experiment on quark-detection in the basement of the Physics Department at Stanford University. Swann was not informed of this test in advance, but he agreed to attempt it.

To Puthoff's amazement, Swann was actually able to perturb the output of the heavily shielded magnetometer. Furthermore, Swann went on to "remote view" the interior of the apparatus, providing a drawing that described reasonably accurately its construction. Puthoff wrote up these observations and circulated them to some of his scientific colleagues.

A couple of weeks later, Puthoff had a visit from two people with CIA credentials. They told him that there was increasing concern at the CIA about the level of effort in Soviet parapsychology that was being supported by Soviet security organizations. In other words, they were worried about Soviet psychic spying capabilities. They asked Puthoff if they could have the opportunity to carry out some simple experiments themselves under Puthoff's oversight and he agreed. These experiments involved hiding objects in a box and asking Swann to try and describe the contents of the box. Swann's results were impressive enough to the CIA people that in short order Puthoff had a $50,000 remote viewing research grant from them, for which he enlisted the involvement of a laser colleague Russell Targ who had an interest in the paranormal.

That, according to Puthoff, was the beginning of the CIA remote viewing program. In 1995, the program was "officially ended" by the CIA, who claimed that it did not yield significant results. However, it is much more likely that these activities continue under the cover of "black projects" completely hidden from any public view.

The scientists Puthoff and Targ were truly dumbfounded by Swann's remote viewing abilities. Swann showed them that he could observe what was going on at a remote location that was identified to him only by its geographic latitude and longitude map coordinates. When Swann proposed trying this, they did not believe it was possible, given the fact that map coordinates are just a man-made construct used for convenience in finding points on a map. But to their great surprise Ingo was able to "go" to a remote location that was given to him with only latitude and longitude map coordinates.

Here is the remote viewing experiment that was most impressive to Puthoff and Targ in terms of what Swann was capable of, as described in their book "Mind-Reach: Scientists Look at Psychic Abilities":

"Ingo," we begin, "a skeptical colleague of ours on the East Coast has heard of your ability to close your eyes and observe a scene miles away. He has furnished us with a set of coordinates, latitude and longitude, in degrees, minutes, and seconds, and has challenged us to describe what's there. We ourselves don't know what the answer is. Do you think you can do it, right off the top of your head?" "I'll try," says Ingo, appearing unperturbed by a request that we, as physicists, can hardly believe we are making.

For us, this is a crucial test. We are certain there is no possibility of collusion between the subject and the challenger. The coordinates indicate a site that is roughly 3,000 miles away, and we have been asked to obtain details beyond what would ever be shown on any map, such as small man-made structures, buildings, roads, etc.

Ingo closes his eyes and begins to describe what he is visualizing, opening his eyes from time to time to sketch a map. "This seems to be some sort of mounds or rolling hills. There is a city to the north; I can see taller buildings and some smog. This seems to be a strange place, somewhat like the lawns that one would find around a military base, but I get the impression that there are either some old bunkers around, or maybe this is a covered reservoir. There must be a flagpole, some highways to the west, possibly a river over to the far east, to the south more city." He appears to zero in for a closer view, rapidly sketching a detailed map showing the location of several buildings, together with some roads and trees. He goes on: "Cliffs to the east, fence to the north. There's a circular building, perhaps a tower, buildings to the south. Is this a former Nike base or something like that?"

A few weeks after Swann's remote viewing description, Puthoff and Targ received a phone call from their East Coast colleague who verified the accuracy of all the details Swann had provided about the physical site three thousand miles away. Needless to say, these two hard-nosed scientists were astounded and believed that they were dealing with a phenomenon inexplicable by the science that they knew.

In 1973 another extraordinary remote reviewing experiment was conducted by Swann, Puthoff, and Targ. The objective was to attempt to have the remote viewer (Swann) "go" to the planet Jupiter and observe what he could at that extraterrestrial location. The reason for this experiment was to test the extreme distance limits of remote viewing in a way that might be scientifically verifiable. Now in 1973 there was a Pioneer spacecraft on its way to Jupiter, Pioneer 10. Pioneer 10 was the very first spacecraft to have a close encounter flyby with Jupiter, which happened in November 1973. So it would be possible to compare the remote viewing results with the observations taken of Jupiter by Pioneer 10. The Jupiter remote viewing experiment was conducted on April 27, 1973, six months before Pioneer 10 was near enough to Jupiter to transmit any data.

The experiment began at 6:00 pm and the first impressions that Swann got of the planet occurred at 6:03 pm. This time difference was noted because it was thought it might relate to the speed of the remote viewing phenomenon. The distance of closest approach between Jupiter and Earth is 588,000,000 kilometers. If it took three minutes (180 seconds) for Swann's consciousness to arrive at Jupiter, then he was "traveling" at 3,300,000 kilometers per second. By way of comparison, the speed of light in a vacuum is 300,000 kilometers per second. So it would seem that Swann "traveled" to Jupiter at approximately 10 times the speed of light!

Here is the actual information that was transmitted verbally from Swann to his transcriber, Hal Puthoff:

6:03:25 "There's a planet with stripes."

6:04:13 "I hope it's Jupiter."

"I think that it must have an extremely large hydrogen mantle. If a space probe made contact with that, it would be maybe 80,000 - 120,000 miles out from the planet surface."

6:06 "So I'm approaching it on the tangent where I can see it's a half-moon, in other words, half-lit/half-dark. If I move around to the lit side, it's distinctly yellow toward the right."

(Hal: "Which direction you had to move?")

6:06:20 "Very high in the atmosphere there are crystals... they glitter. Maybe the stripes are like bands of crystals, maybe like rings of Saturn, though not far out like that. Very close within the atmosphere. [Note: See sketch of ring in the raw data drawing below.] (Unintelligible sentence.) I bet you they'll reflect radio probes. Is that possible if you had a cloud of crystals that were assaulted by different radio waves?"

(Hal: "That's right.")

6:08:00 "Now I'll go down through. It feels really good there (laughs).

I said that before, didn't I? Inside those cloud layers, those crystal layers, they look beautiful from the outside. From the inside they look like rolling gas clouds - eerie yellow light, rainbows."

6:10:20 "I get the impression, though I don't see, that it's liquid."

6:10:55 "Then I came through the cloud cover. The surface -- it looks like sand dunes. They're made of very large grade crystals, so they slide. Tremendous winds, sort of like maybe the prevailing winds of Earth, but very close to the surface of Jupiter. From that view, the horizon looks orangish or rose-colored, but overhead it's kind of greenish-yellow."

6:12:35 "If I look to the right there is an enormous mountain range."

6:13:18 "If I'm giving a description of where I've gone and am, it would be approximately where Alaska is if the sun were directly overhead, which it is. The sun looks like it has a green corona... seems smaller to me.
(Hal: "What color is the sun?")

"White."

6:14:45 "I feel that there's liquid somewhere. Those mountains are very huge but they still don't poke up through the crystal cloud cover. You know I had a dream once something like this, where the cloud cover was a great arc... sweeps over the entire heaven. Those grains which make that sand orange are quite large. They have a polished surface and they look something like amber or like obsidian but they're yellowish and not as heavy. The wind blows them. They slide along."

6:16:37 "If I turn, the whole thing seems enormously flat. I mean, if I get the feeling that if a man stood on those sands, I think he would sink into them (laughs). Maybe that's where that liquid feeling comes from."

6:18:10 "I see something that looks like a tornado. Is there a thermal inversion here? I bet there is. I bet you that the surface of Jupiter will give a very high infrared count (?), reading (?)

(Hal: "Reading... inaudible sentence.)

"The heat is held down."

6:19:55 "I seem to be stuck, not moving. I'll move more towards the equator. I get the impression that that must be a band of crystals similar to the outer ones, kind of bluish. They seem to be sort of in orbit, permanent orbit, down through another layer farther down which are like our clouds but moving fast. There's another area: liquid like water. Looks like it's got icebergs in it, but they're not icebergs."

6:22:20 "Tremendous wind. It's colder here, maybe it's because there's not a thermal inversion there."

6:23:25 "I'm back. OK." (Hal: "Very interesting.")

"The atmosphere of Jupiter is very thick. I mean ... (Ingo draws) ... Explanation of drawing: This is what appears to be a hydrogen mantle about 100,000 miles off the surface. Those here are bands of crystals, kind of elements. They're pretty close to the surface. And beneath those are layers of clouds or what seem to be prevailing winds. Beneath that is the surface which I saw was, well, it looked like shifting sands made out of some sort of slippery granulated stuff. And off in the distance, I guess, to the East was a very high mountain chain 30,000 feet or so, quite large mountains. I feel these crystals will probably bounce radio waves. They're that type.

Generally, that's all."

Swann's "trip" to Jupiter was only 23 minutes in length. However, he reported some startling things. He said that Jupiter had a ring around it, something like the rings of Saturn. This caused Hal Puthoff to wonder if Swann had gone to the wrong planet. It also caused Puthoff's astronomer colleagues to scoff, since no rings around Jupiter had ever been seen by Earth telescopes, and additionally the Pioneer 10 Jupiter flyby later that year did not show any Jupiter rings. But, and this is a very interesting "but", the later Voyager probes of Jupiter in 1979 with their much better photographic resolutions than Pioneer 10, did indeed show that there was a ring around Jupiter. So Swann's remote viewing observation was actually correct. I find this to be quite remarkable.

More startling than the ring, however, was Swann's report that Jupiter had a solid core beneath its cloud layers. He said that there appeared to be solid "mountains" and liquid-appearing regions. Now this made the astronomers in 1973 really derisive, since at that time the consensus was that Jupiter was totally gaseous, with no solid core. Yet, things have changed between 1973 and the present. Astronomers now keep open the possibility of a solid core because it might be related to the intense magnetic field that surrounds Jupiter. In 2016 the NASA Juno probe reached Jupiter and one of its main tasks is to determine whether or not Jupiter has a solid core. If it does, the solid must be solid hydrogen and/or helium, and possibly also liquid forms of these elements. Preliminary results from the Juno probe appear to suggest that this is indeed the case. Wouldn't it be interesting if Ingo Swann's 1973 remote viewing observations about Jupiter were proven right in this regard?

In addition to the work that Puthoff and Targ did with Ingo Swann, they also investigated the remote viewing abilities of other subjects. Their results with three other subjects, Uri Geller, Pat Price, and Hella Hammid, were published in the distinguished scientific journal Nature in 1974 (R. Targ and H. Puthoff, "Information transmission under conditions of sensory shielding", Nature, vol. 251, 18 October 1974, 602-607). The conclusions of their published Nature article were the following:

"From these experiments we conclude that:

A channel exists whereby information about a remote location can be obtained by means of an as yet unidentified perceptual modality.

As with all biological systems, the information channel appears to be imperfect, containing noise along with signal.

While a quantitative signal-to-noise ratio in the information-theoretical sense cannot as yet be determined, the results of our experiments indicate that the functioning is at the level of useful information transfer.

It may be that remote perceptual ability is widely distributed in the general population, but because the perception is generally below an individual's level of awareness, it is repressed or not noticed."

This last conclusion from Targ and Puthoff's Nature article is most interesting. In their studies, they were able to show that many people have an innate capability to exhibit the remote viewing phenomenon. Perhaps even you and I.

Let us now move to a discussion of telekinesis.

We begin with poltergeist phenomena. Poltergeist is a German word meaning "noisy ghost", but poltergeist activities do not involve the actual appearance of a ghost. Most reports of poltergeist manifestations involve noises or movements that have no immediate or verifiable cause. Situations include inanimate objects being picked up or moved, noises such as knocking, rapping, or human voices, and even physical attacks on human beings in some relatively rare cases.

In the 19th century, the most important and best documented case of poltergeist phenomena is associated with the famous medium Daniel Dunglas Home. Descriptions provided by witnesses of the phenomena that occurred in his presence are impressive indeed. In Home's presence, large and heavy objects such as tables were suspended in mid-air with no possible means of support. Superb musical arrangements were played on an accordion Home held in only one of his hands, with the other end of the accordion seemingly moving by itself. Finally and most spectacularly, many witnesses reported Home was able to levitate himself and move around freely in the air with no visible means of support.

Of significant importance is the fact that the psychic phenomena displayed by Daniel Dunglas Home were studied scientifically by Sir William Crookes. William Crookes was one of the most distinguished scientists of the nineteenth and early twentieth centuries. He was both a physicist and a chemist, and the discoverer of the chemical element thallium. Crookes also invented the radiometer and the cathode ray tube. He served as President of the British Royal Society, the Chemical Society, the Institution of Electrical Engineers, and the Society of Chemical Industry. Crookes was elected a Fellow of the Royal Society in 1863, received the Royal Gold Medal in 1875, the Davy Medal in 1888, the Sir Joseph Copley Medal in 1904, and the Order of Merit in 1910. He was knighted for his scientific achievements in 1897. To sum up, William Crookes was indisputably a world-class scientist of his day.

Crookes became interested in spiritualist phenomena in 1869. His original motivation was to debunk such phenomena by making rigorous scientific observations of them. It was in this context that he became involved with the spiritualist D.D. Home, and began to conduct experiments on the spiritualist phenomena Home displayed. Crookes published a summary of his experimental observations with Home in the January 1874 issue of the Quarterly Journal of Science. Here are some of his first-hand scientific observations of phenomena that occurred under carefully controlled conditions in Crookes' own house:

"The instances in which heavy bodies, such as tables, chairs, sofas, etc., have been moved, when the medium has not been touching them, are very numerous. I will briefly mention a few of the most striking. My own chair has been twisted partly round, whilst my feet were off the floor. A chair was seen by all present to move slowly up to the table from a far corner, when all were watching it; on another occasion an arm chair moved to where we were sitting, and then moved slowly back again (a distance of about three feet) at my request.

On five separate occasions a heavy dining-table rose between a few inches and 1 1/2 feet off the floor, under special circumstances which rendered trickery impossible. On another occasion a heavy table rose from the floor in full light, while I was holding the medium's hands and feet. On another occasion the table rose from the floor, not only when no person was touching it, but under conditions which I had prearranged so as to assure unquestionable proof of the fact.

The most striking cases of levitation which I have witnessed have been with Mr. Home. On three separate occasions have I seen him raised completely from the floor of the room. Once sitting in an easy chair, once kneeling on his chair, and once standing up. On each occasion I had full opportunity of watching the occurrence as it was taking place. . . . The accumulated testimony establishing Mr. Home's levitations is overwhelming.

I speak chiefly of Mr. Home, as he is so much more powerful than most of the mediums I have experimented with. But with all I have taken such precautions as to place trickery out of the list of possible explanations.

It is obvious that a "medium" possesses a something which is not possessed by an ordinary being. Give this something a name. Call it 'x' if you like. Mr. Serjeant Cox calls it Psychic Force. This is the force to which the name of Psychic Force has been given by me as properly designating a force which I thus contend to be traced back to the Soul or Mind of the Man as its source."

Crookes ascribed these phenomena to the action of a scientifically unknown "Psychic Force". The scientific community rejected the validity of these experiments, but Crookes, the world-class scientist, had absolute confidence in the reality of his scientific observations of these effects until the day he died.

Perhaps the most famous and well-documented recent poltergeist case is that of the Rosenheim Poltergeist, which took place in Rosenheim, Bavaria. Equipment in the office of a lawyer was observed to operate by itself from summer 1967 to January 1968.

The lights in the office were reported to have turned off and on by themselves, telephones to have rung without anyone apparently calling, photocopiers to have spilled their copier fluid, and desk drawers to have opened without being touched. Post clerks installed instruments that recorded numerous phone calls which were never made. Within five weeks the instruments recorded roughly 600 calls despite the fact that all the phones in the office were disabled. In October 1967 all the office light bulbs went out simultaneously with a loud bang. Pictures on the wall were actually filmed rotating around their hooks. And finally, a heavy filing cabinet is reported to have been pushed across the floor by some invisible force.

The police and the electric company were both called in to try and determine the source of the poltergeist phenomena, but were unsuccessful. Then, a team of well-known scientists was asked to research the phenomena in search of an explanation. They installed cameras and recording devices and were able to determine that the poltergeist events only happened when a nineteen-year-old recently hired secretary by the name of Annemarie Schneider was present. It was thus concluded that Miss Schneider was somehow catalyzing the phenomena, but they were unable to discover how. In the end, the poltergeist phenomena ceased completely when Ms. Schneider was dismissed from the law office.

As was previously described, Ingo Swann not only demonstrated clairvoyant remote viewing abilities, but also telekinesis abilities as well. At the American Society for Psychical Research, he was able to affect the temperature of an isolated and sealed thermistor. At the Stanford Research Institute, he demonstrated the ability to influence the signal generated by an isolated and sealed magnetometer.

What other individuals have exhibited significant telekinetic abilities? The name that immediately comes to mind is Uri Geller and his psychokinetic spoon-bending ability. Geller was born in Israel in 1946 and here is how Geller described his first spoon-bending experience in the late 1950's in his autobiography:

"One time my mother had made some mushroom soup. There was good white bread with the soup, and I dipped the bread into it and ate. Then I started eating the soup with my spoon. I'm left-handed, so I held the spoon in my left hand and took several sips of the soup. My mother was standing by the kitchen stove. I was lifting a full spoonful up to my mouth, when suddenly the bowl of the spoon bent down and spilled hot soup into my lap. Then the bowl of the spoon itself fell off. I was left there holding the handle."

Geller was in the Israeli army at the time of the 1967 Arab-Israeli war. He experienced significant personal combat as a foot soldier and was seriously wounded, but he fully recovered. After he was discharged from the army, he needed to establish a means of making a living. Since he was an outgoing person and had a talent for performance, Geller began to give public demonstrations of metal-bending in various locations within Israel. He stated that having an audience seemed to help him with his metal-bending abilities. However, at one point Geller said his manager urged him to include magician's tricks in addition to his metal-bending demonstrations so as to lengthen the performance and make it more interesting to the viewing public. This he reluctantly did, but in retrospect he said it was a very big mistake on his part, because many people came to believe his metal-bending abilities were in actual fact just magician's tricks as well.

So Geller was making a living as a small-time stage performer at various locations in Israel. But then he came into contact with Dr. Andrija Puharich in November 1971, an event that changed his life dramatically. Puharich was a U.S. medical doctor who also had a great interest in paranormal phenomena. He had heard about Geller's stage shows through the grapevine and became so interested that he traveled from the U.S. to Tel Aviv in Israel to meet Geller in person. He wanted to personally conduct some scientific experiments to evaluate Geller's abilities. This is Puharich's description in his book "Uri: A Journal of the Mystery of Uri Geller" of his initial interaction with Geller:

"My first experiment was to see if Uri had the power to move a magnetic compass needle solely by mental effort. I had two liquid-filled compasses as the test instruments. Uri had never before tried to move a compass needle, so he was very unsure of himself. Before the tests began he gave me permission to search his body for any hidden devices; I found nothing. On the first try, after some seven minutes of concentration, Uri was able to move a compass needle sixteen degrees clockwise. We both felt that this was not impressive, but that he did have potential in this area.

Then I tested his power to "bend" a thin stream of water falling from a water tap when his hand was brought near it. This is purely an electrostatic effect, which anyone can bring about with an electrically charged plastic comb, but very few people accomplish it solely with a finger. Uri was able to bend the water stream when he brought his dry finger near the stream of water. But he could not bend it when his finger or hand was wet with water; wetting his skin seemed to neutralize the electrical charge on his skin.

On the twenty-fourth I started an additional series of tests. I was interested to find out whether Uri could control his mind energy in a narrow beam, or whether he used his energy in a kind of shotgun "scatter beam." My experiment was a simple one. I prepared five wooden matches of equal length and weight and placed them in a long row, end to end. The matches were on a glass plate monitored by a movie camera. Uri's task was to concentrate on the five matches and then try to move any match or group of matches that I selected.

On the first try Uri was able to make the match that I selected move forward some thirty-two millimeters. On succeeding tries he was able to move any match that I selected while the others remained stationary. When moved by his Mindpower, the matches always moved by jumping forward like a frog jumps. I concluded from these tests that Uri could in fact control the beam spread of his mental energy."

The experiments he conducted with Geller impressed Puharich enough that he made arrangements for Geller to come to the U.S. so that scientists could do more controlled experiments on him. In October 1972, Uri Geller visited the Stanford Research Institute to allow Hal Puthoff and Russell Targ to scientifically investigate his alleged spoon-bending abilities. Their objective was to have Geller demonstrate that he could bend spoons without physically touching them himself. In other words, what they wanted to do was to have the spoon be physically located in a sealed and evacuated bell jar, and then observe its bending under the remote action of Geller's mind.

That evening at an informal get together at Uri's Palo Alto residence, Geller was able to bend metal rings that were supplied by the SRI researchers, but not without being able to touch them. Upon leaving the residence after that evening of demonstrations, Puthoff and Targ made the following unexpected observation (from their book "Mind-Reach: Scientists Look at Psychic Abilities"):

"As Hal and I walked down Uri's driveway to our car, we observed a stop sign quite logically placed at the end of the driveway, which intersected a busy cross street. What was illogical was the unusual condition of the sign, which had been supported by the usual five-foot iron stand. The sign, however, was now only two feet off the ground. That was because its support had been bent and twisted to form three complete loops around an imaginary center of rotation, as if to form a spiral slide about the right size for a mouse. As there was no possibility that we would have missed such an object as we entered Uri's house, the twisting must have occurred during our eight-to-midnight bending session. It was difficult to imagine how such a neat job could have been done without the use of heavy machinery."

However, Puthoff and Targ were never able to get Geller to perform a controlled scientific spoon-bending demonstration under remote conditions where Geller did not have any physical contact with the spoon. Yet they were able to observe Geller's ability to modify the weight of an object that was sitting on a precision weighing balance, using only the power of his mind. This object was a one gram weight located inside an aluminum can sitting on a balance, with the whole arrangement covered by a glass bell jar. Geller's mental efforts produced gains and losses of weight on the order of one gram, which was well outside the noise level of the weight measurements. Puthoff and Targ had no physical explanation as to how Geller might have performed this feat.

It should be mentioned that the telekinesis abilities of Uri Geller have been roundly denounced by magician and professional skeptic James Randi. However, I have examined Randi's claims in some detail and found them to be seriously lacking in many respects. Randi is not a scientist and I take the scientific assessments of well-qualified scientists such as Hal Puthoff and Russell Targ to be the truth. Magic tricks cannot withstand rigorous scientific investigations.

Telekinetic effects and particularly metal bending have been investigated scientifically by the British physicist John Hasted, who has written an entire book entitled "The Metal-benders" about his scientific investigations of this phenomenon. Hasted was the head of the experimental physics department at Birkbeck College of the University of London. Interestingly, the famous theoretical physicist David Bohm was also a colleague of Hasted's.

Hasted first became aware of the phenomenon of mental metal-bending through the activities of Uri Geller and Geller's association with the Stanford Research Institute. Hasted and Bohm initially met with Geller in February 1974 in London. Since they knew that some people had claimed Geller was simply a very good magician, they took precautions in advance of their meeting. In particular, Hasted brought along with him four of his own brass latchkeys that were very difficult to bend by hand. Hasted then gave Geller the latchkeys to attempt a metal-bending experiment. Here is his account:

"Geller was quite happy with the keys, and at once took one in each hand, holding it lightly between the forefinger and thumb; I did not take my eyes off them once, not even for a moment. I can affirm that I did not see Geller's other fingers touch the keys (except at pick-up) and that he did not move them more than about an inch from the table surface; they were in my field of vision the whole time. Nothing happened for about forty seconds, and then Geller put the keys flat on the tables about two inches apart and stroked them gently, one with each forefinger. All the time Geller was talking, but I never took my eyes off the two keys and I am certain they never left the table for a surreptitious bend to be performed. After one more minute's stroking, the end of each key started to bend slightly upwards, one (the one stroked by his right forefinger) distinctly more than the other. The angles were 11 degrees and 8 degrees, as measured afterwards."

In another demonstration by Geller, Halsted observed the bending of a metal spoon:

"Geller held the handle and did not touch the bend. Within a few seconds, and under my close scrutiny, the bend in the spoon became plastic. It quickly softened so much that the spoon could be held with one end in either hand and gently moved to and fro. I had never seen Geller produce a really plastic bend before, and I asked him to hand

the spoon to me in one piece. .... I could sense the plasticity myself, by gently moving my hands. It was as though the bent part of the spoon was as soft as chewing-gum, and yet its appearance was normal. ..... As carefully as I could, I laid it on the desk. It was not appreciably warm. I did not dare touch the bent part for fear of breaking it, and it lay on the desk apparently in one piece for a few minutes; but on attempting to move it I was unable to prevent it from falling apart, a 'neck' having developed."

In another example, Geller was able to bend a piece of molybdenum metal without touching it:

"A sudden event observed in an early session of Uri Geller in my laboratory was the bending without touch of a disc-shaped single crystal of molybdenum of about 1 cm diameter. ...... Physicists David Bohm, Ted Bastin, Jack Sarfatt and also Brendan O'Regan were present as witnesses. .... I took the crystal from its box and put it absolutely flat on the plate. Sarfatt extended his hand a few inches above the crystal and the other objects on the plate. Geller moved his hand above Sarfatt's, until a tingling sensation was reported by the latter. Geller tried to 'concentrate his action', and it was suddenly seen by the observers that the crystal had changed its shape, and was now slightly bent, through an angle of about 20 degrees. ...... But I was absolutely certain that neither Geller nor anyone else had touched the crystal since I placed it on the metal plate; nor did he drop anything on the metal plate.

I replaced the crystal in its box, which I returned to my pocket; a physical examination of the crystal would be necessary. I eventually found that a physical property (the magnetic susceptibility) of the crystal was anomalous. ....

Skeptics had a field-day on the basis of this account, and even now it is doubtful if many readers who remember it will be much influenced by my own version. But I myself was impressed by what I had seen, and was reasonably certain that it could not have been a piece of conjuring. This is partly because conjurors do not know about how to change the physical properties of very pure molybdenum; nor could it have been known just what investigation I was going to make."

The metal-bending phenomena that Hasted observed with Geller inspired him to begin an extensive scientific investigation of English children who had also exhibited metal-bending abilities. He employed sensitive scientific equipment to measure and monitor the strains associated with metal bending in real time as they happened. In addition, he did not allow his child metal-benders to touch any of the metal items during his experiments.

At this point I should point out that I am a materials scientist by training and know a good deal about the conditions and mechanisms that are required to permanently bend metals. Let me describe metal bending in a simple descriptive way. Take a strip of aluminum metal that is 1/8 inch thick by 1/2 inch wide by 7 inches long and try to bend it using your two hands. What you will do is put your two thumbs underneath the strip and hold the ends of the strip on top with your fingers; then you will exert a bending force on the strip with your hands. This is what materials scientists call "four-point bending". For the dimensions of the aluminum strip specified, most people should be able to bend it at least a little.

Now when the strip is bent, the aluminum metal in the top portion (called the convex surface) stretches in length. It is termed as being in tension. The bottom portion of the strip (called the concave surface) shortens in length and is termed as being in compression. You may ask how the metal can stretch or compress. It does this by the sliding motion of the atomic crystal planes in the metal, a process that is called "dislocation motion" (dislocations are localized re-arrangements of the atomic planes that allow these planes to slide over each other). Atomic crystallographic sliding occurs and the aluminum metal strip forms a bent shape. This process is called plastic deformation bending and has the characteristic that the strip remains bent after you stop applying the force with your hands.

Now what if you try to do the same thing with a strip of steel having the same dimensions?
Steel is a much stronger metal than aluminum and, unless you are extremely strong, you will not be able to bend it with your hands even as hard as you may try. You will exert the greatest force that you can,

but the steel strip will not permanently bend. It may temporarily show a slight springy-type bending, but when you release the force, the strip will become straight again. This process is called elastic bending. You were not able to bend the steel because you could not exert enough force to start the atomic crystal planes sliding one over the other.

The force that you exert on a metal strip depends on the dimensions of the strip, its width, thickness, and length. For a given metal strip of a certain length, the greater its thickness and width, the harder it becomes to permanently bend it. For example, if the 7 inch aluminum strip were 1/2 inch thick and 3/4 inch wide, you would probably not be able to bend it with your hands alone.

Having gone through this simplified description of the metal bending process, we now go back to describe the experiments of Hasted.

Hasted placed what are called resistive strain gauges on the metal pieces that were to be bent by his child subjects without their touching them. Such gauges are just a thin, narrow, long metal strip that is folded into a compact configuration that can be glued onto the metal pieces. When a force is applied to the metal piece, these gauges elongate in their length and in doing so change their electrical resistance. This change in electrical resistance can be measured with an electronic circuit and the resistance change related to the amount of change in length of the surface of the metal piece (the "strain" that occurs on its surface). It is a very quantitative and accurate way to measure the elastic strain and the onset of plastic strain in a metal piece that is being subjected to a force.

Remarkably, Hasted's strain gauge results established unequivocally that metal pieces were being plastically deformed by his child metal-benders without their touching them in any way. Furthermore, rather than being strictly a bending phenomenon, the strain gauge results showed that the deformation appeared to be more like a plastic "churning" of the metal itself, because the measured metal strains were significantly different in both magnitude and direction from those expected during a straightforward bending process. He speculated that the observed deformation phenomena were possibly related to a temporary lowering of the force required to cause the metal to deform by plastic deformation. The yield force of metals can be made to decrease quite dramatically if they are heated. However, Hasted found no evidence that the local temperatures of the metal pieces were elevated, so it appears that a localized heating effect was not responsible.

In his book, Hasted also described his interactions with French scientists who analyzed the metal-bending abilities of a Parisian by the name of Jean-Pierre Girard. Girard exhibited metal-bending abilities that appear to have been greater than those of Uri Geller. Specifically, Girard was able to deform thick (5/8 inch diameter) round aluminum alloy metal bars that were 10 inches in length. Here is Hasted's description:

"I was present at a session at which Girard was filmed in a deformation requiring 23 Nm (note that Nm refers to the scientific newton-meter unit of mechanical torque)*; the protocol was good, and, as the video-record shows, the manual force was minimal. It is Girard's custom to hold one end of a bar of circular cross-section in his right hand and pass his left hand slowly over the other end for minutes at a time; he then lays the bar down on a flat surface and rests for a short while. After repeated attempts deformation gradually appears; even a small deformation can be observed if the bar is rolled on a flat surface."*

Girard was hooked up to an EEG machine during the metal bending event. The EEG recorded high levels of alpha waves at a frequency of 10 Hz. Such alpha waves typically occur during relaxation and the onset of sleep, but Girard's recorded heartbeat at the time was 160 beats per minute.

The French research with Girard concentrated on analyzing the metallurgical aspects of paranormal metal-bending. All of the bars bent had their deviations from straightness very accurately measured. The metal microhardness, which is an index of the dislocation structure in the bent metal, was measured at a large number of points in the bar. The residual strain profile in the bar after bending was measured using x-ray diffraction techniques. Bent regions of the bar were analyzed with both scanning and transmission electron microscopy to determine any changes in the metal crystallographic substructure. Electron microprobe analysis was performed to determine the local chemistry of regions of the bar.

The metallurgical analyses indicated that the paranormally bent metal was different from that of normally bent metal. Specifically, the residual stress patterns in the bars bent by Girard were drastically different from those patterns in a normally bent bar. These results suggested that the elastic strain portion of the deformation was essentially eliminated in the paranormally bent bars. It was as if the bars started bending plastically at very low levels of applied force. This would suggest that significant local softening was occurring at the bent regions by a mechanism other than a localized high temperature, since there was absolutely no evidence of localized temperature increases. It was postulated that large numbers of plastic-deformation-producing dislocations were somehow being produced in the paranormally bent metal and that their subsequent motion to produce deformation was being made abnormally easy by some unknown mechanism. But how such things could happen in the metal was totally unclear to the scientists. And it is also a scientific mystery to the materials scientist who has written this book.

It is evident from the above scientific studies of paranormal metal-bending that the phenomenon of telekinesis is a real one and not a magic trick. This clearly needs to be explained on some suitable basis, given the controlled and detailed scientific observations that have been made of these effects.

I am very astonished that the scientific picture of the real world around me is very deficient. It gives a lot of factual information, puts all our experiences in a magnificently consistent order, but is ghastly silent about all and sundry that is really near to our heart, that really matters to us. It cannot tell us a word about red and blue, bitter and sweet, physical pain and physical delight; it knows nothing of beautiful and ugly, good or bad, god and eternity.

Erwin Schrodinger

Non-Physical Consciousness:

Every scientist knows that he or she is a conscious person, but other than that, very little is known by science about consciousness. I myself cannot be totally certain about the reality of the people and things that surround me, but I at least know for sure that I am real. I am conscious that I exist as a real entity. As Descartes most famously and succinctly put it in 1644 "cogito ergo sum" (I think, therefore I am). I have a consciousness that exists and is capable of thought. I know with certainty that I have thoughts and feelings that are my own, that are part of my "inner life". This is a quite basic aspect of reality for every human being.

But just what is this "I" that I am so sure about. Close your eyes, look inside yourself and try to sense the origin of your most basic, most personal "I". Try to find the root of your "I" feeling. If you do this, you will see that you cannot locate your "I". It eludes you when you try to define it with any action, desire, memory, or thought. What this tells you is that the "I" can be experienced, but it cannot be "seen". Fundamentally, the "I" is the observer, the experiencer that is there prior to any conscious content. Another way to express this is that the "I" is identically equal to awareness.

In another thought experiment, consider that you are in a sensory deprivation chamber. It is totally dark and completely silent. Your body is floating in a warm liquid, so you have no sensory touch inputs. There are no smells and no tastes. Your five senses are completely shut down. In this state, you are totally isolated from the outside world. The only things that you have are your thoughts and feelings. However, even these mental states come and go. But the one thing that remains is your awareness - your awareness is your “I”.

Is your “I”, your awareness, produced simply by physical brain function, or is it something else entirely, something non-physical? Every night during your non-REM sleep, your conscious “I” seems to disappear, only to reappear during REM sleep and when you awake. If someone knocks you unconscious, your conscious “I” disappears temporarily until you regain consciousness. The same is true if you are anesthesized. So clearly brain function is a necessary condition for a conscious “I”. However a central question is whether the “I” also exists when your brain is unconscious or non-functional.

What is the reality of my own personal consciousness? Where does my consciousness reside and what is its nature? My personal experience is that my consciousness seems to reside in my head, somewhere just behind my eyes. The head is a logical place to perceive consciousness. After all, it is the site of the brain where our five senses are integrated into conscious experience. So it seems reasonable that I would locate my consciousness there rather than someplace else in my body, say my knee for example.

What goes on with my consciousness during a typical day of my current lifestyle (you might also call this a day in the life of “I”)? The first thing that happens is that I wake up from the night’s sleep. For a short period of time, I may remember some aspects of the dream I was dreaming just before waking, but after a while the dream memories fade. The need to perform certain bodily functions rises into my consciousness, but only when their call becomes somewhat urgent. Actually, I have little awareness of most of my body functions unless I choose to focus on them. Moving my head and my limbs, breathing, blinking my eyes are all relatively automatic.

During the day, legions of thoughts pass through my head. Some are mundane and regular. I need to take the dog out when he comes in proximity with his "I really must go" little whine. In the morning when I first take him for his walk, I feel the cool breeze and breathe the fresh morning air. I see the sun about to rise and marvel at the magnificence of the morning sky. My vision takes in the plants, flowers, and shrubs that surround our dwelling place.

I make myself breakfast and then have a cup of coffee while I sit down at my computer and review the emails that have accumulated during the night. My thoughts are centered on them and on the news that I review through my computer screen. I think about the things I want to try and accomplish during the new day.

My wife wakes up and we exchange morning pleasantries. I go and perform the rituals of making our bed and shaving and washing my face, while my wife bustles around with her morning chores.

Then I go back to my computer and begin performing my intellectual work of the day. At the present moment, this involves thinking about the content of the book that I am writing, and then trying to express my thoughts in a semi-coherent way. Other days it may involve different intellectual pursuits. My thoughts roam around the ideas and concepts that I wish to convey in my book. This may also involve searches on the computer for information that is related to the concepts that I am attempting to formulate and shape in my mind. These thoughts are of a much more abstract character than my everyday thoughts.

At various times during the day, my consciousness becomes occupied with more mundane, analytical things. I have bills to pay and chores to do around the house. Since I am a scientist, part of my time is devoted to attempting to stay current with the latest new developments that are happening in the realm of science. I track and read scientific journals on a daily basis.

During an average day, my consciousness often dwells on memories both recent and from long ago. Recent memories are near-term things such as "when did I last take the dog out" or "when will my wife return from her errands". But the long-term memories are another matter. When I drift into these memories, it is truly amazing to me how much I can remember from such long ago times. I can remember minute details of places and events that happened when I was a child. I see again in my mind the layout of both the interior and exterior of the home where I first lived more than 65 years ago. It all comes back so vividly. How do these memories enter into my consciousness, and from where?

In any given day, events perturb my consciousness from the outside world that are completely unexpected and unanticipated. The phone rings and I need to take some action based upon the call. Or I run into a person and have an unexpected interaction with them. It seems that such things enter my consciousness from outside my "inner space". They are happening because something external to me produced them. What is the nature of that externalness?

Sometime every day I spend time in meditation. This is an activity that I have been doing for many years and I must say that I believe it has had a positive influence on expanding the level of my consciousness. To enter the meditative state, I sit in a chair in a quiet place, close my eyes, and then go through a mental procedure that is designed to clear my mind of all the thoughts that it normally has. When I achieve the non-thought state (which I am now able to do during most of my meditative sessions thanks to years of practice) my consciousness essentially "blanks out". This state has a resemblance to non-REM sleep but it differs in that I still seem to retain a sense of awareness, but it is awareness without thought. I am quite certain that I am not asleep. After a period of time, typically 30-40 minutes, my thoughts will return spontaneously and I come out of deep meditation. During the time I am in it, I have absolutely no memory of where "I" was and what "I" was doing. Where was my consciousness during meditation?

Each day there are moments when I experience personal qualia, my subjective consciousness experiences. For example, the calendar on my wall is currently showing a photo of a beautiful red flower with a magnificent dragonfly sitting on it. These miracles of nature inspire me. I seem to have inherited an eye for art somewhere, even though I have trouble making even simple drawings on my own. I look up and see the painting of an island landscape that my daughter painted when she was a child and it delights my eye, as do the paintings that my artistically gifted wife produces.

I try and get some rigorous physical exercise almost every day because I spend a lot of time sitting in a chair at my computer and I need to make up for this. Sometimes I go down to the exercise room in our condo building and use the treadmill or stationary bike, and sometimes my wife and I go for long walks on the beautiful beach that is not far from our home. Except for the beach walks, I listen to music when I exercise. The music resonates with my consciousness, takes my mind away from the exercise routine, and makes me feel happy.

In the evenings I have dinner and conversation with my wife and then retire again into my study for another session of intellectual pursuits. The computer and internet have been a great aid to me in terms of expanding my personal consciousness into very many areas. I am a voracious reader and the bookshelf in my study is crammed to overflowing with books. I seek out books on science, spirituality, consciousness, roots of religions, the paranormal, and the mysterious and unexplained.

Before retiring for the evening, I typically watch something on television to mentally relax. Then I climb into bed and apply a meditative technique to fall asleep quickly. During the cycles of my non-REM sleep, I have absolutely no memory of what may or may not have taken place, or of my awareness. In the cycles of REM sleep, I have dreams where I am one of the characters in the dream action, and these dreams often incorporate elements of my conscious memory. Then I wake up the next morning and the next day in the life of my consciousness begins.

The reason that I have gone through this perhaps slightly tedious description of a day's worth of my consciousness is not to bore you but rather to illustrate the very subjective nature of consciousness. These are some of the thoughts and feelings, the qualia, which are associated with my consciousness every day. They certainly appear to be unique personal thoughts and experiences that seem almost impossible for a chemical biological machine to produce. The question is how do they occur?

At the present time, many of the people who investigate the nature of consciousness are of the opinion that there are two aspects to it. These are termed access consciousness and phenomenal consciousness. Access consciousness is associated with information in our minds that is accessible for verbal reporting, reasoning, and the control of behavior. This is the more mechanistic aspect of consciousness that is generally termed the "easy problem of consciousness" and is thought to be associated with brain mechanisms.

But then there is phenomenal consciousness. It is the subjective aspect of consciousness associated with the subjective "qualia" that we all experience, such as the things I described in my day in the life. Phenomenal consciousness is described as the "hard problem of consciousness" because it is much harder to conceive how it occurs.

The term "hard problem of consciousness" was coined by consciousness researcher David Chalmers at a famous meeting on the subject held in Tucson, Arizona in 1994. It is essentially this: How do physical processes in the brain produce subjective experiences? In other words, how are the first-person "I" experiences (i.e. qualia) produced by third-person brain events. Chalmers formulation of the "hard problem" has defined intellectual discussions of consciousness since he first put it forward in 1994.

The people who study consciousness fall into two camps. The first group seeks solutions through materialist explanations of brain function for both access and phenomenal aspects. We will call this group the "consciousness monists". The second group thinks that while access consciousness is related to brain function, phenomenal consciousness involves something more than just brain material, something much less tangible than the mass of neurons in the brain. This group we term the "consciousness dualists".

Consciousness monists say that we are nothing more than body and brain. Our consciousness is essentially a result of brain function. They argue that there is no such thing as spirit or soul. The most famous recent monist has been Francis Crick, the Nobel Prize winner for the discovery of the structure of DNA. Crick put forward the "astonishing hypothesis". Basically, the "astonishing hypothesis" says (as expressed by Crick):

"that 'you', your joys and your sorrows, your memories and your ambitions, your sense of personal identity and free will, are in fact no more than the behavior of a vast assembly of nerve cells and their associated molecules."

In other words, your consciousness is essentially the integrated activities of your nerve and brain cells. The central problem with the monist approach is that no one has yet been able to scientifically establish where or how brain cells and their associated brain centers integrate the consciousness. One cannot identify where in the brain the consciousness is located or how consciousness is assembled in the brain. Nor can monists effectively explain the subjective "I" qualia.

There are two general monist concepts of the brain and consciousness. The first suggests that specific groups of neurons in the brain are associated with specific conscious experiences. That was Crick's view. This concept surmises that there is one set of brain neuron groupings for, say, the conscious experience of the beauty of a painting, and another different set of neuron groups for, say, the conscious abstractions of quantum mechanics. The second approach conceives that consciousness is derived from a more generalized increase in the brain's neural activity. However this view says nothing about what creates consciousness in the brain, but only what controls the level of consciousness. The first approach might be described as the "neuron quality" viewpoint, while the second as the "neuron quantity" concept.

Consciousness dualists, on the other hand, argue that first-person "I" experiences such as qualia are associated with a mind function that is somehow separate from just the materialistic firing of collections of neurons in the brain, but which controls the patterns of neuron firing in some subtle way. David Chalmers, who first brought the "hard problem" to the forefront is the most prominent current consciousness dualist.

The most famous early consciousness dualist was Rene Descartes, the formulator of the Cartesian coordinate system. Descartes said the body and the spirit (soul) coexist together in the living person. It is the spirit that is the conscious entity and that embodies the mind. Descartes' concept is termed "the ghost in the machine". The body and the brain are physical entities, while the spirit and mind are non-physical entities. Thus, they are fundamentally different from each other and this raises the key scientific problem with the "ghost in the machine", which is: How does the "ghost" interface with the "machine"? This is certainly a very valid scientific question. How do our sensory inputs from the physical world outside get to the spirit, the mind, so that the mind can think about them and feel them? Similarly, how do the thoughts and decisions generated by the mind translate into actual physical actions? Descartes postulated that this interfacing took place in the pineal gland at the center of the brain.

Present day consciousness dualists reject Descartes' spiritual explanation of consciousness in favor of more scientifically-based approaches, many of them associated with the mysteries inherent in quantum mechanics that I have previously described. They seek a quantum mechanical mechanism that can couple to the mechanics of brain cell functioning to provide explanations for the subjective functioning of the mind.

The various views of these two consciousness groups have been very nicely summarized in the book "Conversations on Consciousness" by Susan Blackmore. In it, Blackmore conducted interviews with twenty prominent philosophers and scientists who have studied consciousness in depth. She herself has done considerable work in this area and must certainly be considered a group member. She would probably classify herself as a consciousness monist, but perhaps she is one with underlying doubts and a certain fondness for Buddhist concepts.

Blackmore formulated a list of standardized questions about consciousness to pose to each of her interviewees. The first question was: What is the problem? In other words, why is consciousness such a difficult subject to get one's hands around as compared to other scientific subjects? This question was posed to try and define the difficulties with consciousness, and also to have the interviewees identify themselves with either the monist or the dualist consciousness groups.

Blackmore also asked the interviewees for their views about "zombies". In the consciousness community, the topic of zombies revolves around the following thought experiment. Is it possible for there to be a being who looks exactly like you and responds exactly like you in terms of speech, externally expressed thoughts, and external actions, but who has no inner, subjective life?

Another of Blackmore's questions was: Do you believe in life after death? Blackmore herself felt that a personal life after death would be incompatible with a scientific view of the world. She was interesting in knowing what the other interviewees thought about this, probably to compare their responses to her own monist view. Clearly, monists would answer in the negative, while dualists would be more open to the possibility.

All the above questions that Blackmore presented to her interviewees have an important bearing on the issues associated with the reality of consciousness. I will now elaborate on a few of the responses that she received, starting with the monists.

Blackmore interviewed the monist Francis Crick shortly before his death in 2004. When Blackmore asked Crick why consciousness was such a difficult problem, he replied:

"There's no easy way of explaining consciousness in terms of known science. The easiest way to talk about the problem is in terms of qualia. For example – how can you explain the redness of red in terms of physics and chemistry?"

Crick agreed that the hard problem was the crux of the difficulty in understanding consciousness. He went on to indicate that he was looking for brain neural correlates that correspond to what we are conscious of. Particularly, he was seeking to determine the difference in brain activity when a person was conscious as compared to when they were unconscious. In other words, he wanted to establish the brain mechanisms for the conscious mind in the hope that this would reveal a materialist source of qualia. But one got the clear impression from his interview that he did not have a rationale for where in the brain to even begin looking.

Then there was the interview with the well-known monist Daniel Dennett. Dennett is a professor of philosophy at Tufts University in Massachusetts and director of the Center for Cognitive Studies there. He is also the author of a book with the audacious title "Consciousness Explained". He takes the position that there is no hard problem, that qualia simply do not exist, that they are actually a delusion that people experience for reasons that are unclear. When Dennett expresses the "I" word, he takes it to relate to the "agent" that he argues is the whole body of an individual. Oddly enough, Dennett expressed the view that he, the "agent", had a free will:

"The model that we want to have for free will is of an agent that is autonomous, not in some metaphysical sense, but in the sense of being able to act on the reasons that matter to the agent, and who's got the information that is needed to act in a timely fashion."

The problem I have with Dennett is that he is a philosopher and not a scientist like Crick. There seems no phenomenological basis for his rejection of the existence of qualia, which I unequivocally know I have. I am in no way delusional when I experience them, they seem fundamental to me. But then, as Dennett stated: "*Philosophy is what you do when you don't yet know what the right questions are to ask.*"

Now let us see what a few dualists have to say about consciousness. We begin with David Chalmers, the person who coined the term "the hard problem" in 1994. Chalmers was born in Australia in 1966. He first began studying mathematics but then became fascinated with the topic of consciousness and earned a Ph.D in philosophy and cognitive science from Indiana University. Following a number of years as Director of the Center for Consciousness Studies at the University of Arizona, he then returned to Australia to take the position of Director for Consciousness Studies at the Australian National University. Here is how Chalmers described the hard problem in his conversation with Susan Blackmore:

"The heart of the science of consciousness is trying to understand the first person perspective. When we look at the world from the perspective of science, we take the third person perspective. We see a subject as a body with a brain, and with certain behaviour. We can be terribly objective, but something very important about being a human being is left out. As human beings we all know that it feels like something, from the inside. We have sensations, thoughts, and feelings. ...... The hard problem is the question of explaining how it is that all this is accompanied by subjective experience. That seems to go beyond any mechanistic question about how the various behaviours and functions are produced."

Interestingly, Chalmers stated that he agreed with Descartes' famous statement about consciousness, cogito ergo sum (I think, therefore I am). For Chalmers, dealing with the subjective nature of consciousness requires a paradigm shift. He believes that consciousness must be treated as a fundamental of nature, along with other fundamentals of nature. Only by taking such an approach can a bridge be built between the third-person science of brain function and the first-person nature of consciousness.

When Chalmers was asked if he believed in free will, his response was that he didn't know what free will meant. And when questioned about what happens to consciousness after death, he said that he would probably cease to exist, but it would be very nice if he were completely wrong about this.

Roger Penrose and Stuart Hameroff have coupled their respective areas of expertise in an attempt to develop a scientific basis for Chalmers' view of consciousness as a fundamental aspect of nature. Penrose is a professor of mathematics at the University of Oxford. He was knighted for his contributions to science, and is well-known for his 1989 book "The Emperor's New Mind" which suggested links between consciousness and quantum mechanics. Hameroff is an anesthesiologist, a medical field closely associated with human consciousness. He is a professor of Anesthesiology and Psychology at the University of Arizona.

Penrose feels that the link between science and the hard problem of consciousness lies in the area of quantum mechanics. Perhaps the reason for his feeling is that both quantum mechanics and consciousness subjectivity are, at their root, "strange" in the sense that they seem to transcend physical reality as we currently understand it. Being a mathematician, he bases his belief on Godel's famous incompleteness theory of mathematic logic as follows:

"I'm saying that the Godel argument tells us that we are not simply computational entities; that our understanding is something outside computation. It doesn't tell us it's something unphysical, but there's a crucial thing that's missing, which has to do with quantum mechanics. ...... Quantum mechanics is the most obvious place where we don't know enough about physics. Where do you see non-computability in physics? You don't seem to see it anywhere else. So this, therefore, is presumably where it is."

Having made the assumption that the essence of consciousness lies in quantum mechanics, the next scientific step is to try and establish a link between quantum mechanics and brain mechanisms. This is where Hameroff's expertise comes in. Hameroff has been studying protein structures called microtubules in the internal structure of brain cells. It is in the biochemistry of the tiny microtubules that he thinks quantum mechanics might have the possibility of influencing brain mechanics.

Blackmore asked Hameroff what he thought happens to consciousness after death and this was his response:

"When the quantum coherence in the microtubules is lost, as in cardiac arrest, or death, the Planck scale quantum information in our heads dissipates, leaks out, to the Planck scale in the universe as a whole. The quantum information which had comprised our conscious and subconscious minds during life doesn't completely dissipate, but hangs together because of quantum entanglement. Because it stays in quantum superposition and doesn't undergo quantum state reduction or collapse, it's more like our subconscious mind, like our dreams. And because the universe at the Planck scale is non-local, it exists holographically, indefinitely. Is this the soul? Why not."

So there you have an encapsulation of the views of a few of the current leading lights on the subject of consciousness, both monists and dualists. Into which camp does your intuition take you? Consciousness is indeed the hardest of hard problems.

There have been two very interesting experimental scientific investigations related to the subject of consciousness. The first is the Global Consciousness Project and the second are studies conducted to probe consciousness effects on the quantum mechanical double-slit experiment.

Let us describe the Global Consciousness Project. The predecessor of the Global Consciousness Project was the Princeton Engineering Anomalies Research (PEAR) program at Princeton University. One of the primary areas of research was to determine if human consciousness could influence random number generators. A random number generator is an electronic device that generates a random sequence of numbers; the simplest to generate is just a random sequence of the binary numbers 0 and 1. If one has a random sequence of 0's and 1's, the mean value of a large sequence will be ½ because just about as many 0's will come up as do 1's if a large enough sample is taken. This is the electronic equivalent of randomly flipping a coin and measuring the occurrence of heads or tails, except that it is much more truly random than any physical coin flipping experiment.

The PEAR program demonstrated with high statistical significance that a human being could use their consciousness to "will" the appearance of more 1's than 0's, or more 0's than 1's in a sequence of binary bits. The effect was however small, of the order of 0.0005 per binary bit. That is to say, if one had a random sequence of 100,000 binary bits, you would normally expect 50,000 of them to be 0's and 50,000 of them to be 1's. However, when people tried to "will" say more 1's to occur, then the observation was that the random number generator produced 50,050 of the 1's. This was a small but statistically quite significant effect that could be produced by one human being acting alone with their consciousness.

The Global Consciousness Project was begun in 1998 to determine if much larger numbers of people could have more of an effect on a random number generation scheme that was global in nature. To this end, over 60 sophisticated random number generators (RNGs) are located at the present time in diverse locations around the globe. There are presently RNGs sited in Europe, the US, Canada, India, Fiji, New Zealand, Japan, China, Russia, Brazil, Africa, Thailand, South America, and Australia. These RNGs generate binary random number sequences (0's and 1's) through the completely random process of quantum tunneling in an electronic device. There can be no doubt that the RNGs are producing truly random binary number sequences in the absence of any external physical influence, since significant protections are in place to isolate these devices from any external electronic effects. The RNGs run around the clock and transmit their data via the internet to a central collection point. At this collection point, the data are analyzed to determine if there are any deviations from global randomness at any given point in time.

The central hypothesis of the Global Consciousness Project is the following: Periods of collective emotional or attentional behavior in widely distributed populations will correlate with deviations from expectation in a global network of RNGs.

Thus, the investigation seeks to correlate global randomness with high-impact, high visibility events that occur from time-to-time in the world. 390 such events have been evaluated as of the year 2011. Some of these events are:

U.S. Embassy bombings in Africa on August 7, 1998
JFK Jr. death on July 17, 1999
Millennium Event on January 1, 2000
Terrorist attacks on September 11, 2001
9/11 one year anniversary on September 11, 2002
Columbia space shuttle disaster on February 1, 2003
Catastrophic tsunami on December 26, 2004
Hurricane Katrina landfall in New Orleans on August 29, 2005
Saddam Hussein's execution on December 30, 2006
Benizar Bhutto assassination on December 27, 2007
Chinese earthquake on May 12, 2008.
President Barack Obama inauguration on January 20, 2009
Earthquake in Haiti on January 12, 2010

Osama Bin Laden killed on May 2, 2011
Hurricane Sandy hits East Coast on October 29, 2012
End of the Mayan Calendar, December 21, 2012
Boston Marathon bombing, April 15, 2013
Robin Williams suicide, August 11, 2014
Paris terror attacks, November 13, 2015

Here are the Global Consciousness Project results for one particularly traumatic worldwide event, the September 11, 2001 terrorist attacks on New York and Washington DC. The measurement of global non-randomness began to become significant about one hour after the collapse of the second World Trade Center building. Presumably this was the time that the maximum level of global awareness and concern took hold. The global non-randomness then continued at a high level until September 16, when the published analysis of the data was terminated. The probability that the measured level of global non-randomness on September 11 was an actual, true phenomenon was determined to be 99.95% through a rigorous statistical evaluation of the global RNG data.

The cumulative global non-randomness data obtained by the Global Consciousness Project for the 390 global events analyzed have shown that this is a real effect to a probability of 99.999999999%. Clearly the effect is real. What is completely missing is a scientific explanation for the observed phenomenon. Right now there is absolutely no explanation as to how a global awareness/consciousness of a major global event can have such a dramatic non-randomness effect on the electronic generation of world-wide random number generators which, according to our current scientific paradigms, should be producing absolutely random numbers.

The scientist Dean Radin has conducted landmark experiments related to the effect of conscious observation on the quantum mechanical double-slit experiment. Recall that in the double-slit experiment, particles such as electrons and photons can exhibit particle-like or wave-like behavior depending on whether or not an observation is made of which slit individual electrons or photons actually passed through. When there is no observation, these entities act as waves. But when their passage through one or the other of the slits is actually observed at the time they are passing through, then they exhibit particle-like behavior. This is the essence of the particle-wave duality of quantum mechanics, as well as the act of observation collapsing the quantum mechanical Schrodinger wave function. Nobel Prize winning scientist Richard Feynman said that the double slit experiment was at the heart of quantum mechanics.

Here is a description of Radin's experiments and results (Dean Radin, et.al. "Consciousness and the double-slit interference pattern: Six experiments", Physics Essays, vol. 25, No. 2, 157-171 (2012)) . The double slit experiment was completely sealed inside a closed metal box. It consisted of a helium-neon laser, a double-slit arrangement through which the laser beam could pass through, and a specialized ccd camera detector that was employed to record the diffraction pattern after the laser beam had passed through the double-slit. The output from this apparatus was the intensity of the diffraction peaks of the laser light after it passed through the double-slit.

Now sitting two meters away from this assembly was a person who was instructed to keep a vision of the double-slit in their mind, so that they were effectively acting as an observer of the laser light passing through the double-slit.

The experiment was to see if the observer using his consciousness to observe the double-slit, could then reduce the measured intensity of the laser light diffraction peaks. This was taken to be equivalent to having a detector at the double slit that could record which slit individual photons were actually passing through. Such observation would be expected to favor particle-like behavior over wave-like behavior.

So basically, the experiment was set up to measure the diffracted laser power both when the observer was concentrating his consciousness on the double-slit, and when he was not. If a significant difference were to be measured, then this would indicate that the observer's consciousness was actually affecting the quantum mechanical phenomena that were happening at the double-slit. Said another way, it would indicate that the consciousness of the observer was able to cause the wave function of the laser photons to collapse to that of particles.

A number of people were employed as observers in these experiments. These people were divided into two groups, people who practiced meditation on a regular basis and those who were not meditators. The thinking was that the meditators would be better able to concentrate their consciousness on the double-slit than would be the non-meditators. The initial results indicated that the meditators were able to reduce the measured wave diffraction power coming through the double-slit, but that the non-meditators were not able to do so. This was attributed to an enhanced ability of meditators to maintain their concentration on the double-slit.

So it appeared that meditational observers located two meters away from the experimental apparatus could indeed influence the results of the experiments with their conscious minds. And the experiments indicated that the observed effect was a 5-Sigma result.

Now what is the meaning of a 5-Sigma result? Basically a 5-Sigma result means that the probability of the observed result being due only to chance is 1-in-3,500,000. A 5-Sigma result says that the observed result is very, very likely to be true. For comparison to the present case, the discover of the Higgs Boson made at the Large Hadron Collider was also a 5-Sigma result.

So what we have here is apparently very solid scientific proof that consciousness can have an influence on quantum mechanical events!

Radin examined the effect of proximity of the observer to the double-slit experimental equipment. To do this, the observers were set up to "observe" the double-slit through the internet. So they were physically quite removed from the experimental equipment. 2000 internet sessions were held with human observers in this remote study. In addition, there were 2000 non-human "robot" internet sessions that were made, for comparison to the human internet observations.

It was observed that while the robot internet observers had no effect on the double-slit, the human internet observers did have a significant influence. Furthermore, the actual physical distance between the internet human observers and the experimental equipment had no effect. Distance did not matter at all, whether the people were across town or across the world.

Now one might say that what Radin observed is not a quantum effect because with a continuous laser, one is dealing with a gazillion photons per second. Therefore Radin repeated the experiment, but now using experimental equipment where only individual photons were passing through the double-slit (yes, it is possible to do this experiment with individual photons).

Using individual photons passing through the double-slit, the result was the same. A person's consciousness could act as the observer when an individual photon approached the double-slit, thus collapsing its quantum mechanical wave function so that it behaved as a particle and thus passed through only one of the slits. Radin's experimental results with the double-slit experiment are indeed profound. They provide evidence that consciousness plays a role in creating the reality that we experience.

Space is not empty. It is full, a plenum as opposed to a vacuum, and is the ground for the existence of everything, including ourselves. The universe is not separate from this cosmic sea of energy.

David Bohm

Consciousness as the Fundamental of the Non-Physical:

Science currently says that invisible factors have a major influence over our physical universe.

Dark Matter and Dark Energy are presently considered to make up 95% of our physical reality, but we have absolutely no knowledge as to what these things are. They are called "Dark" because they are invisible to all our scientific instruments of characterization. Science says that Dark Matter constitutes 25% of our physical reality, Dark Energy constitutes 70% of our physical reality, while the ordinary matter and energy that we presently think we understand account for only 5% of our physical reality. So at present we can scientifically observe only 5% of what our reality actually is.

Dark Matter was first experimentally detected in the 1970's when it was observed that the velocity of stars in galaxies did not reduce as expected based on their distances from the galactic center. The inference was that the galaxies were actually encased in a volume of Dark Matter that was invisible in the sense that it did not emit any electromagnetic radiation. We cannot see it, but we infer that it is there because it has a gravitational influence on the ordinary matter that we can see. The only interaction Dark Matter exhibits with ordinary matter is gravitational.

We are much more certain what Dark Matter is not than we are what it is. First, it is dark, meaning that it is not in the form of stars and planets that we see. Observations show that there is far too little visible matter in the universe to make up the 25% required by the observations. Second, it is not in the form of dark clouds of normal matter, matter made up of particles called baryons. We know this because we would be able to detect baryonic clouds by their absorption of radiation passing through them. Third, dark matter is not antimatter, because we do not see the unique gamma rays that are produced when antimatter annihilates with matter. Finally, we can rule out large galaxy-sized black holes on the basis of how many gravitational lenses we see. High concentrations of matter bend light passing near them from objects further away, but we do not see enough lensing events to suggest that such objects make up the required 25% dark matter contribution.

Since the 1970's, scientists have been making heroic efforts to determine what Dark Matter might be, but thus far to no avail. Dark Matter does not interact with ordinary matter or ordinary energy in any way, other than gravitationally. It is still Dark to our understanding. One possibility being explored is that Dark Matter is composed of "weakly interacting massive particles" (WIMPs).

The detection of WIMPs is being pursued in two large experiments, LUX and PandaX-II experiments. Here, a detector is constructed deep below ground with a massive target to increase the odds of an interaction with the Dark Matter that exists in our Galaxy. In the case of LUX and PandaX-II, the dark matter particles are expected to leave behind traces of light that can be detected with sophisticated sensors.

The heart of both LUX, located in South Dakota in the US, and PandaX-II, situated in Sichuan, China, is a time-projection chamber. This consists of a large tank of ultrapure liquid xenon—250 kg at LUX and 500 kg at PandaX-II—topped with xenon gas. A particle (Dark Matter or ordinary matter) that enters the chamber and interacts with a xenon atom in the liquid generates photons (by scintillation) and electrons (by ionization). The photons produce a signal, $S1$, which is read by photomultiplier tubes located at the top and bottom of the tank. The electrons are coaxed into the gaseous portion of the detector by an electric field where they induce a second round of scintillation and a signal $S2$. The pattern of $S1$ and $S2$ signals is expected to be different when the xenon interacts with a Dark Matter particle than with an ordinary particle, which is what allows scientists to distinguish between two such events. To reduce the background signal from ordinary particles, both LUX and PandaX-II are buried deep underground to provide protection from cosmic rays. In addition, the use of ultrapure materials in the construction of the experiment cuts the background contributed by radioactive emissions.

Thus far, no evidence of WIMPs have been detected in these sophisticated experiments. And so the scientific community continues to speculate about the nature of Dark Matter.

Dark Energy is even more mysterious than Dark Matter. Dark Energy is considered to be the energy that is contained in the vacuum of space. Dark Energy is thought to be very homogeneous, not very dense and is not known to interact through any of the fundamental forces other than gravity. Since it is quite rarefied, un-massive - roughly 10^{-27} kg/m^3 - it is unlikely to be detectable in laboratory experiments. The reason Dark Energy can have such a profound effect on the universe, making up 70% of universal density in spite of being so rarefied, is because it uniformly fills all of "empty" space.

Dark Energy acts on ordinary matter in a manner opposite of gravity. Instead of an attractive force, Dark Energy produces a repulsive force on the matter of the universe. It is this repulsive force that is considered to be the reason that the universe is presently accelerating in its expansion. Furthermore, since Dark Energy is a property of space and because space itself is expanding, therefore the amount of Dark Energy is increasing with this expansion of space.

One explanation for Dark Energy is that it is one of the properties of the so-called space vacuum. Albert Einstein was the first person to realize that empty space is not nothing. Space has amazing properties, many of which are just beginning to be understood. The first property that Einstein discovered is that it is possible for more space to come into existence. Then one version of Einstein's gravity theory, the version that contains a cosmological constant, makes a second prediction: "empty space" can possess its own energy. Because this energy is a property of space itself, it would not be diluted as space expands. As more space comes into existence, more of this energy-of-space would appear. As a result, this form of energy would cause the universe to expand faster and faster. Unfortunately, no one understands why the cosmological constant should even be there, much less why it would have exactly the right value to cause the observed acceleration of the universe.

Another explanation for how space acquires energy comes from the quantum theory of matter. In this theory, "empty space" is actually full of temporary ("virtual") particles that continually form and then disappear. But when physicists tried to calculate how much energy this would give empty space, the answer came out wrong – and wrong by a lot. The number came out 10^{120} times too big. That's a 1 with 120 zeros after it. It's very hard in physics to get an answer that bad.

Another explanation for Dark Energy is that it is a new kind of dynamical energy fluid or field, something that fills all of space but something whose effect on the expansion of the universe is the opposite of that of matter and normal energy. Some theorists have named this "quintessence," after the fifth element of the Greek philosophers. But, if quintessence is the answer, we still don't know what it is like, what it interacts with, or why it exists. So the mystery continues.

Space presently contains two major aspects that are invisible and unexplained. Perhaps they are associated with another level of reality. It is clear that both Dark Matter and Dark Energy can presently be classed as non-physical in nature.

Let us now put forward the hypothesis that consciousness is the most basic fundamental of reality and pervades all things both physical and non-physical. Consciousness can be conceived as a field of non-physical energy that pervades all of space. In this sense, consciousness might appear to be somewhat similar to what scientists currently call Dark Energy. It may also be related to the zero point energy field proposed by quantum mechanics. One may call this all-pervading field the field of Universal Consciousness.

Here is what Max Planck, one of the founders of quantum mechanics, had to say about consciousness:

"I regard consciousness as fundamental. I regard matter as derivative from consciousness. We cannot get behind consciousness. Everything that we talk about, everything that we regard as existing, postulates consciousness."

Another famous physicist, Prof. John Wheeler, regarded consciousness as a fundamental. Wheeler, after a long intellectual evolution working in physics, attempted to approach physical reality not as something "out there" which is passively described by observers, but to see it as a genesis through conscious dialogue between observers/participants and physical reality, so that the universe emerges as a special articulation of the relationship between consciousness and physical reality.

Here is a quotation from Wheeler on this subject:

"The brain is small. The universe is large. In what way, if any, is it, the observed, affected by man, the observer? Is the universe deprived of all meaningful existence in the absence of mind? Is it governed in its structure by the requirement that it gives birth to life and consciousness?"

What is consciousness? Philosophy and science have been attempting to come to grips with this question since their beginnings, but this is still very much an open question.

What then is consciousness? Basically, for human beings consciousness is self-awareness of existence. A human being knows that he or she exists. Descartes said "I think, therefore I am". I personally prefer the following version: "I am, therefore I think".

Everything in the universe is pervaded by consciousness. There is a philosophical term for this: panpsychism. What is panpsychism? Panpsychism argues that everything that exists in our physical universe possesses some degree of consciousness. This includes both living as well as non-living (inert) things. The concept of panpsychism was put forward by the Greek philosophers Thales and Plato, and more recently by the modern philosopher William James.

Consciousness can be considered to be composed of two aspects: form and content. In the final stage of his enlightenment under the Bodhi tree, the Buddha found that at the root of all things was consciousness and that form was a necessary part of consciousness.

Form may be thought of as the complexity of an existing thing. There are a vast number of forms in the material universe that we currently know, ranging from subatomic particles, photons, atoms, molecules, gases, liquids, solids, viruses, bacteria, single-celled organisms, multiple-celled organisms, plants, insects, animals, and human beings.

The most rudimentary content of consciousness is the ability of a form to sense and interact with its immediate environment. The highest form of consciousness that we currently know in our physical world is the self-awareness and abstract thinking ability of the human being.

An electron is a physical unit with mass and charge. A photon is a unit with no mass and no charge. These things are aspects of the form of these physical species. The consciousness content of these species gives them a range of interactive ability. Conscious content can vary over extremely vast limits. For sub-atomic particles, their consciousness content permits them only to sense and interact with their very local environment. At the other end of the spectrum, the consciousness content of human beings allows humans to be able to think abstract thoughts such as why they exist and the nature of reality.

Starting with the smallest things that science currently knows, this argues that protons, neutrons, electrons, and photons all possess a fundamental consciousness, however vanishingly small. An electron has a fundamentally simple form in the spectrum of our physics. The consciousness content of an electron knows when it encounters another electron since their negative charges repel one another. Similarly when the electron encounters a positive proton, it is attracted to it. A photon also has a fundamentally simple form and a fundamental content of consciousness in that it can interact with electrons and atoms.

An atom has a consciousness form that is more complex than a sub-atomic particle since it is composed of more than one sub-atomic particle. A hydrogen atom is the combination of a proton and an electron. The consciousness content of an atom is also more complex than that of a sub-atomic particle because an atom can interact with other atoms as well as protons, neutrons, electrons, and photons. Thus, an atom has a higher consciousness level than that of a sub-atomic particle.

One might ask the question: Is the consciousness level of a large atom like uranium greater than that of a small atom such as hydrogen? I expect not. The form of the uranium and hydrogen atoms are the same since they are both combinations of protons, neutrons, and electrons. And the consciousness content of the two types of atoms are the same; they can sense and interact with protons, neutrons, electrons, photons, and other atoms in their immediate vicinity.

Let's now consider molecules. Molecules are made up of atoms, so their consciousness form is greater than that of individual atoms. The water molecule H_2O contains two hydrogen atoms and one oxygen atom. Is the consciousness content of a molecule larger than that of an atom? It would seem so. Molecules can interact with other molecules in addition to atoms and sub-atomic particles. As with atoms, the consciousness level of molecules does not increase with their size.

The perception of non-living things such as fundamental particles, atoms, and molecules as being totally inert things without consciousness is incorrect according to panpsychism. Anything composed of matter has some level of consciousness, however rudimentary. In nature, rocks have consciousness, air has consciousness, water has consciousness.

Do the things that humans manufacture from matter also have consciousness? My computer certainly has a form, but it is not a form that occurs naturally in nature. It is a form that is a construction, a creation if you will, of human beings. My computer was created by humans. But the various elements of my computer are all composed of atoms and molecules. The brain of my computer, the microprocessor, controls a vast and elaborate flow of electrons from one place to another.

Because the constituents of my computer all possess consciousness, this would logically argue that my computer also has consciousness, at a form and content at least as high as that of its highest consciousness constituent which in the case of the computer would be a molecular consciousness. But one might argue that the computer's consciousness level should be higher than this because its consciousness content is higher. The computer takes input information, coordinates the vast movements of electrons to process this information, and then provides output information.

This poses the issue about the possibility of self-aware artificial intelligence. Clearly, present day computers can perform some selected tasks much more rapidly and extensively than the human brain. And with time, computers will undoubtedly excel humans in a great many other brain-related tasks. Is there the possibility that at some point a seemingly inert computer system could someday achieve self-aware consciousness? It is a very intriguing question indeed.

Let us now proceed into the realm of so-called living things and begin with the DNA molecule.

The DNA molecule contains the molecular codes for the formation of all living things. Human DNA is composed of 3 billion molecular base pairs configured in the double helix structure. Rather interestingly, the human DNA molecule is not the largest found in nature. The largest known DNA molecule is associated with a flower called paris japonica which has 152 billion base pairs. However, the consciousness levels of all DNA molecules are the same, regardless of their size.

But the DNA molecule has something that other molecules do not possess, the ability to code and transmit information to other molecules. One might argue that this higher content level of DNA gives it a consciousness level that is higher than all other molecular species.

We next consider viruses, the boundary between non-living and living things. Viruses are essentially a DNA (or RNA) molecular core encapsulated by a protein molecular shell. A virus is an integrated assembly of molecules. Yet a virus particle can be born (i.e. chemically formulated), reproduce itself (it needs to do this by invading a bacterium or cell), and die (i.e. be disrupted in chemical configuration). The consciousness level of a virus is greater than that of an individual molecule because the consciousness form of a virus is made up of more than just one type of molecule. In addition, the consciousness content of a virus is greater than that of a molecule because the virus can reproduce itself within bacteria and living cells.

What about bacteria and individual living cells? Bacteria and individual living cells are similar in consciousness form. They are composed of a nucleus of DNA, surrounded by other molecular structures of various specialized functions, with everything contained inside a cell wall. The consciousness level of bacteria and individual living cells is greater than that of a virus because the consciousness form and content are greater.

There is a gradient of consciousness levels for living things just as there is a gradient of consciousness levels for non-living things. The consciousness of a virus might be said to be the bottom level of living things. The consciousness of a bacterium is larger than that of a virus and the consciousness of a single-celled amoeba is greater than that of a bacterium. The consciousness of a multi-celled plant is higher than that of an amoeba, the consciousness of an insect is larger than that of a plant, and the consciousness of an animal is more extensive than that of an insect.

There are certain animals that appear to possess a self-aware consciousness. Animals such as orangutans, chimpanzees, gorillas, dolphins, elephants, orcas, monkeys, and magpies have all been observed to pass the mirror test. In the mirror test, a mark is placed on the face of these animals and then they are allowed to view themselves in a mirror. Self-aware animals are seen to recognize in the mirror that there is a mark on their faces, so they know that they are seeing their own face in the mirror. It's interesting that domestic animals such as dogs and cats do not pass the mirror self-awareness test. This is rather surprising given that these domestic animals interact so extensively with their human owners.

My own personal feeling is that all animals have a self-awareness nature of consciousness, even if they do not respond to the mirror test. Is my pet dog self-aware? Yes, I'm certain that he possesses that level of consciousness. He knows he exists, he expresses his needs, he seems to dream during sleep, he feels pain. I think this is the case for all animals, even the lowly rat.

Now what about the human animal?

The human body is composed of approximately 40,000,000,000,000 (40 trillion) human cells. Each of these cells has a life cycle, interacts with its environment, and undergoes reproduction. Each individual cell has an extremely small level of consciousness as compared to the consciousness of the overall human.

One might be tempted to ask the question: Is the human body consciousness equivalent to simply the sum of the individual consciousnesses of the 40 trillion human cells in the human body? Definitely not. If this were true, it would imply that smaller humans have a lower consciousness level than larger humans just because of the differences in the absolute number of cells in their respective bodies. This is patently absurd.

The human body form is indeed composed of the vast array of cells that constitute it, but the human body consciousness content is vastly greater than that of individual cellular consciousness because the extent of sensing and evaluating interactions with the environment via the human brain is so much greater for the human body as compared to an individual cell.

Humans certainly possess the consciousness level of self-awareness, but much more than this they are able to think in the abstract, to think about advanced concepts and to construct things in their imagination. Human beings can think about why they exist. I do not believe that the lower self-aware animals have this consciousness capacity.

But let's put this into perspective. In the physical universe it is highly likely there are physical beings that possess consciousness greater than that of humans. For example, there may be self-aware beings on other planets who have a larger number of senses than just the human five and also have larger and/or more sophisticated brain structures with which to process the increased amounts of information provided by these additional senses, as well as perform more extensive abstract thinking.

Astronomical observations have shown that there are probably as many planets in the universe as there are stars. And there are approximately 10,000,000,000,000,000,000,000 stars in the visible universe that we can currently observe with our telescopes. So it is inconceivable that intelligent life does not exist somewhere else in the universe and it probably occurs in a great many places. There may be many intelligent physical beings and many of these may have consciousness levels higher and probably much higher than those of humans.

Consciousness is a part of our universe, so any physical theory which makes no proper place for it falls fundamentally short of providing a genuine description of the world.

Roger Penrose

Possible Nature of Non-Physical Universal Consciousness:

Here I will speculate as to the possible nature of non-physical Universal Consciousness. My speculations are based upon a combination of intuition and knowledge of our current physics.

Now you might say, his speculation about the existence and nature of a non-physical Universal Consciousness seems metaphysical in character rather than having anything to do with our physical reality. However, in this regard it is useful to begin by outlining the speculations that are inherent in an advanced theory of physics, namely string theory.

String theory is presently considered to be the best theoretical formalism for a “Theory of Everything”. This is because it is seen to be the best way currently available to consolidate the theories of quantum mechanics and general relativity.

String theory surmises that the fundamental constituents of everything physical are one-dimensional “strings”. These strings are the building blocks of all matter as well as the physical forces that act upon matter. The origin of string theory is a mathematical formalism developed by the great mathematician Euler in the 18th century. Euler’s formula described the behavior of string-like species.

Strings are considered to be extremely minute one-dimensional packets of energy. The size of a string is taken to be of the order of the

Planck length. Strings can be of two forms, a closed form like a rubber band, and an open form like a cut rubber band. The strings can vibrate in various vibrational states. But these vibrations are taken to be a different form of energy that is not electromagnetic in characteristic. As an analogy, consider the motion of a pendulum. A pendulum swings back and forth. During the center of its swing, it has maximum kinetic energy, but at the end of its swing, the kinetic energy has all been changed to potential energy. This is considered to be a harmonic oscillation of the energy type of the pendulum. Strings are massless quantities, they have no mass only energy. But the nature of this energy is quite ill-defined.

In string theory, both sub-atomic matter particles, termed fermions, and force carrying particles, termed bosons, are considered to be made of strings with different types of energy vibrations. According to string theory, the properties of an elementary "particle"—its mass and its various force charges—are determined by the precise resonant pattern of vibration that its internal string executes. Each elementary particle is composed of a single string and each particle is a single string.

So a fermion such as an electron has one type of string vibration, while a boson such as a photon has another type of vibration. Through Einstein's equation $E = mc^2$, strings of higher energy will produce particles of higher mass. One of the triumphs of string theory was to predict the existence of a particle called a graviton. A graviton is taken to be the force-carrying particle of gravity. So string theory has the potential of uniting the theories of quantum mechanics and general relativity.

But there is a price to be paid for this. In order to be mathematically tractable, there must be 10 dimensions in string theory. These would constitute our 3 physical dimensions plus time, plus 6 other "physical dimensions" that we never experience. These additional 6 dimensions are considered to be so tiny, of the order of the Planck length, and "curled up", which is the reason why we don't experience them directly.

There have been a number of variants of string theory proposed, but now theorists have discovered that they are all variations of what is called M-theory. There seems to be no consensus as to what the "M" stands for. Some theorists say "Membrane", some say "Mother" (as in Mother of all theories), and yet others say "Murky", "Mystery", or "Magic". Perhaps the last is most apt since M-theory requires the existence of an 11th dimension.

There are two major criticisms of string theory. The first is that it has so many potential variants to it, of the order of an incredible 10^{500} possible variations, that because of this it would be virtually certain to be able to describe anything observed in our physical world by selecting the proper variants.

The other major criticism is even more compelling. String theory has not produced any predictions that are testable experimentally, because the strings themselves are so vanishingly small and the extra dimensions required are impossible to access. A theory can only be called a scientific theory if there is some way to experimentally test if it is false. Here is an example of this. Let us consider the "theory" that "all swans are white". Now, we can measure ten swans and find that are they are all white, and even a thousand swans and find that the thousand are all white. But if we find just one swan that is black, then the theory is clearly false. The ability to experimentally falsify a theory is the litmus test of its scientific reality.

It appears that it is experimentally impossible to falsify string theory. This makes some scientists argue that string theory is not science, but rather something in the realm of mathematics and/or metaphysics. Yet the string theorists argue that because their theory is so mathematically elegant and has the potential to unite quantum mechanics and general relativity, that it must be correct even though it cannot be experimentally falsified.

Let us now come back to a consideration of the possible nature of non-physical Universal Consciousness.

We will posit that Universal Consciousness is an all-pervading field of conscious energy that underlies the physical realm. The

vibrations in this field are of the size of the Planck length or smaller so that, as with string theory, they are undetectable in our physical world. The higher the vibrational level, the greater the degree of consciousness. Furthermore, also as with string theory, Universal Consciousness is associated with many higher dimensional levels. The physical realm is contained within the much larger realm of Universal Consciousness, which to us in the physical appears to be non-physical because we cannot detect it.

What is the nature of the vibrations in the Universal Consciousness field? The same question can be asked of the vibrations in string theory. String theorists say that their vibrations are vibrations of energy of the strings, but that is a rather vague description since they do not really know what type of energy is involved. The electromagnetic vibrations of the electric and magnetic fields that we know in the physical realm no longer exist at the scale of the Planck length. Perhaps the best one can say of the vibrations in the Universal Consciousness field is that they are vibrations of conscious energy. But they are not vibrations that possess the characteristics of energy as we know it in the physical, because their vibrational "frequencies" are so much higher than anything we can physically conceive or experience.

I think that there are a number of key aspects that govern non-physical Universal Consciousness. Here are some of what I think these "Laws" might be.

The first is that non-physical Universal Consciousness exists outside of our physical spacetime.

Our physical realm consists of 3 physical dimensions and 1 dimension of time. Einstein incorporated these together into a four-dimensional spacetime.

But what if there was a 4th physical dimension or even more physical dimensions? In our three dimensional world, we know of left-right, up-down, and forward-backward. But we have no concept at all of the nature of a fourth spatial dimension, which, for lack of a better terminology, might be called "in-out". What the dickens could "in-out" be? We haven't the slightest idea until we can actually experience it directly.

If a three-dimensional sphere were to pass through a two-dimensional Flatland, it would first appear to the Flatlanders as a small dot that increased to a maximum size circle and then decreased back to a dot. That is how the Flatlanders were perceive a three-dimensional sphere that passed through their two-dimensional world. Before and after the intersection, the sphere would be completely invisible to the Flatlanders.

Now let's consider a cube passing through Flatland. If the cube approaches Flatland face-on, then its appearance in Flatland will be the sudden appearance of a square, and it will remain the same sized square until its abrupt disappearance from Flatland. If the cube approaches Flatland from an edge, it will first appear in Flatland as a line, which will then change to a rectangle that will increase in size to a maximum, then decrease in size until the cube exits Flatland as a line. Finally, if the cube approaches Flatland from a diagonal, it will enter Flatland as a point, then change into a triangle that increases in size to a maximum, and then the triangle will decrease in size until the cube then exits Flatland again as a point. Again, before and after the intersection with Flatland, the cube will be completely invisible to the Flatlanders.

One might ask the question: How would three-dimensional Spacelanders perceive the passage of a four-dimensional object through their reality? By analogy with the Flatland case, the 4D object would present itself as a three-dimensional shape.

One can get a feel for this by considering the tesseract. In geometry, the tesseract is the four-dimensional analog of the three-dimensional cube. The tesseract is to the cube as the cube is to the two-dimensional square.

All point locations within a four-dimensional tesseract are specified by four numbers rather than just the three in three-dimensional space. While the tesseract can be described with mathematical completeness, it can only be visualized as a three-dimensional form that can best be described as a cube within a cube, where the vertices of the inner cube are connected to the vertices of the outer cube. Another way to visualize the tesseract is this. Just as a three-dimensional cube can be "unfolded" in two dimensions as an array of six squares, so a tesseract can be "unfolded" in three-dimensions as an array of eight cubes.

We can see from the above discussion the fact that higher dimensions will be invisible to lower dimensions unless some intersection occurs, and that the higher dimensional form will be incompletely known in lower dimensional observation. Furthermore, all lower dimensions are contained within the realm of the higher dimensions. So the concept that non-physical Universal Consciousness incorporates four-dimensional spacetime as a subset of itself is a logical one.

Science says that spacetime becomes "granular" at the length scale of the Planck length. It no longer possesses the continuous properties of our normal spacetime. So at the scale of the vibratory Universal Consciousness field, there is no spacetime. There is only the consciousness field.

Our physical spacetime is essentially a subset that is contained within the much larger non-physical Universal Consciousness. Our physical universe is like a cloud in an otherwise clear sky. As suggested by string theory, the non-physical is likely to be higher dimensional than our physical three dimensions.

In the non-physical realm, things are possible that seem impossible in our physical realm. One possible example of this are the knots placed in a closed-loop piece of rope by the 19th century medium Henry Slade.

Here is the account of this phenomenon as observed by the scientist Prof. Johann Zollner, a Professor of Physical Astronomy at the University of Leipzig, and written in his 1882 book "Transcendental Physics":

"We three-dimensional beings can only tie or untie such a knot by moving one end of the cord through 360 degrees in a plane which is inclined towards that other plane containing the two-dimensional part

of the knot. But if there were beings among us who were able to produce by their will four-dimensional movements of material substances, they could tie and untie such knots in a much simpler manner by an operation analogous to that described in relation to a two-dimensional knot.

As one of these effects, I discussed at some length the knotting of a single endless cord. If a single cord has its ends tied together and sealed, an intelligent being, having the power voluntarily to produce on this cord four-dimensional bendings and movements, must be able, without loosening the seal, to tie one or more knots in this endless cord.

Now, this experiment has been successfully made within the space of a few minutes in Leipzig, on the 17th of December 1877, at 11 o'clock A.M., in the presence of Mr. Henry Slade, the American. The accompanying engraving (Plate I.) shows the strong cord with the four knots in it, as well as the position of my hands, to which Mr. Slade's left hand and that of another gentleman were joined. While the seal always remained in our sight on the table, the unknotted cord was firmly pressed by my two thumbs against the table's surface, and the remainder of the cord hung down in my lap.

I had desired the tying of only one knot, yet the four knots—minutely represented on the drawing—were formed, after a few minutes, in the cord. The hempen cord had a thickness of about 1 millimetre ; it was strong and new, having been bought by myself. Its single length, before the tying of the knots, was about 148 centimetres; the length therefore of the doubled string, the ends having been joined, about 74 centims. The ends were tied together in an ordinary knot, and then—protruding from the knot by about 1.5 centims.—were laid on a piece of paper and sealed to the same with ordinary sealing-wax, so that the knot just remained visible at the border of the seal. The paper round the seal was then cut off, as shown in the illustration. The above described sealing of two such strings, with my own seal, was effected by myself in my apartments, on the evening of December 16th, 1877, at 9 o'clock, under the eyes of several of my friends and colleagues, and not in the presence of Mr. Slade.

Two other strings of the same quality and dimensions were sealed by Wilhelm Weber with his seal, and in his own rooms, on the morning of the 1 7th of December, at 10.30 a.m. With these four cords I went to the neighbouring dwelling of one of my friends, who had offered to Mr. Henry Slade the hospitalities of his house, so as to place him exclusively at my own and my friend's disposition, and for the time withdrawing him from the public. The seance in question took place in my friend's sitting room immediately after my arrival.

I myself selected one of the four sealed cords, and, in order never to lose sight of it before we sat down at the table, I hung it around my neck—the seal in front always within my sight. During the seance, as previously stated, I constantly kept the seal —remaining unaltered — before me on the table. Mr. Slade's hands remained all the time in sight; with the left he often touched his forehead, complaining of painful sensations. The portion of the string hanging down rested on my lap,—out of my sight, it is true,—but Mr. Slade's hands always remained visible to me. I particularly noticed that Mr. Slade's hands were not withdrawn or changed in position. He himself appeared to be perfectly passive, so that we cannot advance the assertion of his having tied those knots by his conscious will, but only that they, under these detailed circumstances, were formed in his presence without visible contact, and in a room illuminated by bright daylight.

I reserve to later publication, in my own treatises, the description of further experiments obtained by me in twelve seances with Mr. Slade, and, as I am expressly authorised to mention, in the presence of my friends and colleagues, Professor Fechner, Professor Wilhelm Weber, the celebrated electrician from Gottingen, and Herr Scheibner, Professor of Mathematics in the Uni versity of Leipzig, who are perfectly convinced of the reality of the observed facts, altogether excluding imposture or prestidigitation."

So Prof. Zollner, a very reputable scientist, reported that he personally observed Slade to be able to produce knots in a closed-loop piece of cord, and he was absolutely convinced that no trickery or slight-of-hand was involved in this event because of the precautions that had been made. I would note that no magician has ever been reported to be able to place knots in an initially unknotted closed piece of cord that he did not physically hold in his own hands.

We must presume that this phenomenon actually occurred as Prof. Zollner described. Such an event would be impossible in our three-dimensional reality, so it would seem that a higher dimensional reality was involved in some way. Something non-physical was going on here. So the existence of higher dimensions may be one "Law" of the non-physical.

The famous physicist David Bohm speculated about higher dimensions of reality in his book "Wholeness and the Implicate Order". The idea he put forward is that the specifics of our reality are just a part of a higher reality where everything is innately connected to everything else on a very fundamental level. Bohm took this more encompassing reality to be of a higher dimensional nature. He further postulated that the reality described by our current physics (general relativity and quantum mechanics) is something that is contained within or enfolded into this higher reality. Bohm stated that the physical ordering that we observe is essentially an "enfolded order" that is contained within and manifests out of a greater "implicate" reality under certain conditions. What our current physics describes is "explicate order" in that each physical thing lies only in its specific region of space and time and outside the regions belonging to other physical things. This is the basis for Bohm's new paradigm of "wholeness and the implicate order".

Bohm put forward two specific scientific phenomena that can help in the understanding of what he proposed.

The first is a phenomenon that is observed with the viscous flow of fluids. Consider the experiment where you have two concentric (one inside the other) glass cylinders with a layer of a viscous clear liquid such as glycerine in between the two cylinders. A drop of black insoluble ink is then placed in the viscous liquid and the outer cylinder is turned very slowly so that there is no turbulent mixing of the liquid. What you will observe is that the initial spherical ink particle becomes drawn out into a finer and finer filament shape as the outer cylinder is rotated more and more, until eventually this filament becomes so fine in size that you can no longer see it. From the point of view of your vision, it has effectively disappeared into the liquid as a result of the outer cylinder rotation.

But here comes the interesting part. If you now slowly rotate the outer cylinder in the opposite direction, the ink filament will eventually start appearing again, and with a suitable amount of counter-rotation, the spherical ink drop will be totally reconstituted. So the ink drop that disappeared into the liquid has now been resurrected. Remarkable! Yet, this is a real physical phenomenon that anyone can observe to happen with the right equipment.

Bohm took this experiment to be a way to see how explicate reality, the reality that we experience and that our current physics describes, can be enfolded into a higher reality and extricated from this higher reality under the proper set of conditions. In other words, the implicate order is more fundamental than the explicate order.

To illustrate "undivided wholeness", Bohm evoked the physical phenomenon of the hologram.
A hologram is a three-dimensional image of a three-dimensional object that is recorded as an optical interference pattern on a two-dimensional plate. Holograms are produced as follows.
The three-dimensional object to be imaged is irradiated by a monochromatic laser beam. The beam is split into two parts using a beam splitter. The first half of the beam strikes the object and the scattered light from the object then proceeds to a flat two-dimensional plate. At the same time, the second half of the beam bypasses the object and proceeds directly to the flat two-dimensional plate. When these two beams arrive at the plate, they interfere with each other, producing a two-dimensional diffraction pattern on the plate. This diffraction pattern looks somewhat like TV screen "snow" when there is no channel being received.

Now if you take the same type of laser beam used to create the two-dimensional diffraction pattern and shine this laser beam through the diffraction pattern on the plate, like magic a three-dimensional image of the original object will appear floating in space on the other side of the plate. Furthermore, if you cut the two-dimensional diffraction pattern plate in half and then shine the laser beam through only the one-half plate, you will still reconstruct the entire three-dimensional image, not just one-half of it. In fact, if you cut the plate into many small pieces and shine the laser beam through just one of these small pieces, you will still get the entire three-dimensional image, but with a somewhat lower resolution of features. This is a physical example of Bohm's concept of "undivided wholeness".

What Bohm proposed in his new paradigm is an undivided wholeness of the totality of existence that is present in a dimensionality different from our present physical three-dimensional reality. Our entire universe with its subatomic particles, atoms, molecules, inanimate objects, and life forms is fundamentally an undivided wholeness. These "things" are basically only manifestations of the localized flow (termed holomovement by Bohm) of the wholeness. Finally, Bohm postulated that our consciousness is an integral part of this undivided wholeness.

A second aspect of the non-physical is that conscious thought produces reality.

We have already shown that in quantum mechanics, the act of conscious observation produces the reality of what is observed in the double-slit experiment, the quintessential aspect of quantum mechanical behavior. There are solid scientific experimental results that support this conclusion.

Here is what Prof. R.C. Henry, Professor of Physics and Astronomy at The Johns Hopkins University, said in his book "The Mental Universe":

"A fundamental conclusion of the new physics also acknowledges that the observer creates the reality. As observers, we are personally involved with the creation of our own reality. Physicists are being forced to admit that the universe is a "mental" construction. Pioneering physicist Sir James Jeans wrote: "The stream of knowledge is heading toward a non-mechanical reality; the universe begins to look more like a great thought than like a great machine. Mind no longer appears to be an accidental intruder into the realm of

matter, we ought rather hail it as the creator and governor of the realm of matter."

We surmise that the conscious act of thinking about something in the non-physical produces that something immediately. In the non-physical, conscious thought produces the reality that is experienced.

Another aspect of the non-physical is the instantaneous transmission of thought.

This may be related to the non-local phenomena observed in quantum mechanics, the so-called "spooky action at a distance" described by Einstein.

According to Einstein's Theory of Relativity, the cosmic speed limit is the speed of light in our spacetime physical universe. Although the speed of light, 300,000 kilometers per second, seems very, very fast to we humans, it is actually a relatively slow speed for communications across the physical cosmos.

The distance from Planet Earth to the nearest star from the Sun, Proxima Centauri, is 4.24 light years. So it takes 4.24 years for the light from Proxima Centauri to reach us. Our Sun is located on the outskirts of our Milky Way galaxy and our solar system is about 25,000 light years from the galactic center. And the nearest galaxy to the Milky Way, Andromeda galaxy, is 2,540,000 light years away. Clearly, the speed of light is a very slow way to get around the vast universe.

Thought is an element of consciousness, thought exists within consciousness. Science has experimental evidence of the instantaneous connection of entangled quantum species, the so-called non-locality of quantum mechanics.

Perhaps consciousness and thought are composed of waves with wavelengths of the Planck length or shorter that are not electromagnetic in nature, but are of a different nature. Such waves might have transmission speeds much, much higher than the speed of spacetime light, effectively being instantaneous in transmission.

In the non-physical, linear uni-directional time does not exist, there is only the Now, which encompasses what we in the physical universe consider to be past, present, and future.

Both the theories of quantum mechanics and relativity are insensitive to the direction of time. Their equations work equally well in the increasing time direction as well as in the decreasing time direction. However, they do incorporate the aspect of causality. Causality is the agency that connects one process (the cause) with another process or state (the effect), where the first is responsible for the second, and the second is dependent on the first. While causality is not dependent on the direction (or arrow) of time, it is dependent on the linearity (or passage) of time.

In the non-physical, both past and future events as we perceive them in the physical, all exist simultaneously in the non-physical Now. Time is totally non-linear in the non-physical. Here in the physical, it appears to us that time flows in a linear, one-way direction that we have no control over. However, we perceive physical space quite differently. We can proceed both backwards and forwards in space and indeed go in any spatial direction that we choose. In the non-physical, one can move to any desired point of time that incorporates both the past and the future as we perceive them in the physical. Just as we have the flexibility in the physical to move in space wherever we wish, so in the non-physical the flexibility exists to move wherever is desired into both the past and the future.

The hardest part of this to grasp from the physical viewpoint is how the physical future can be contained as already established reality within the non-physical Now. This seems to violate our physical concept of causality, which of course is a basic tenet of science. Actions in the past are considered to produce their effects in the future. How can this be rationalized?

Perhaps the Many Worlds interpretation of quantum mechanics might provide such a rationalization. The Many Worlds interpretation says that everything that can happen from decisions and actions in the past, does indeed happen in a future that consists of an infinite number of future possible realities. If all possible future realities exist in the non-physical, then all possible past-future connections must also already exist simultaneously. Admittedly, this is difficult for those in the physical to accept as the true nature of non-physical reality, but then again the physical is only as small subset of the non-physical. Our future may be only one of an infinite number of possible futures.

The all-pervading Universal Consciousness field bears a certain resemblance to the quantum mechanical zero-point field.

Recall that quantum mechanics says there is a vast field of energy that permeates the entire physical universe. This field of energy apparently exists outside of our normal space and time, and is considered to be "virtual" in nature. It is a seething configuration of electromagnetic energy of all wavelengths, from the largest possible to the smallest possible wavelength. The energy in the zero-point field would be infinite, were it not that scientists consider the shortest possible electromagnetic wavelength to be the Planck length.

However, because the vibrations present in the Universal Consciousness field are surmised to have "wavelengths" of the Planck length and shorter, they cannot be a part of the quantum mechanical electromagnetic zero-point field. The Universal Consciousness vibrations are something else entirely.

The strings in string theory are postulated to have vibrational modes that contain differing amounts of energy. These vibrations are not electromagnetic in nature, so what are they? String theorists simply say that they are the resonant vibrational patterns of the strings. And what are the strings? Their answer is that this question is meaningless because the strings are the fundamental components of all matter and force-producing particles. The transition is made from strings to matter through the Einstein equation $E = mc^2$.

The vibrations of the Universal Conscious field can be considered to be conscious energy. They constitute a fundamental nature of energy. How can energy be conscious? One can ask the question: What is energy? College freshman physics books grandly state that "energy is the ability to do work". But this definition is completely off the mark.

It says nothing about what energy is, only about what energy does. Science knows about the kinds of things that kinetic energy, potential energy, and electromagnetic energy can do. But what is energy? What is the essence of energy, the truth of energy? In fact, no scientist in the world can answer this simple question. Here is what the famous physicist Richard Feynman had to say about the nature of energy: "*It is important to realize that in physics today, we have no knowledge of what energy is.*"

We posit that energy in its purest form is, in fact, consciousness. The vibratory frequencies of conscious energy are so much higher than those of physical energy, and these consciousness vibrations form the "carrier wave" that is the basis of all physical energy and matter.

Interaction of the Universal Consciousness field with physical reality.

At this point, one must ask the question: How does the Universal Consciousness field interact with the three-dimensional physical reality that we presently experience? The vibrations of Universal Consciousness are probably a different type of energy as we know it, but the physical world is composed of physical dimensional energy.

The Universal Consciousness field exists in a higher dimension than physical reality. As has been pointed out, things that exist in the 4th dimension will be invisible to us in the three-dimensional world. Perhaps consciousness vibrations are higher vibrations of what we know as energy in this physical world. On this basis, Universal Consciousness vibrations are the source of three-dimensional energy.

We postulate that the vibrational frequencies of Universal Consciousness are much, much higher than any vibrational frequencies associated with energy as we know it. On this basis, Universal Consciousness can create energy (and hence also matter) by substantially lowering its vibrational frequency into the range of frequencies that can exist in the three-dimensional world.

How can this lowering of frequency happen? A possible analogy as to how this is possible is associated with the phenomenon of binaural beats.

In acoustics, a binaural beat is an interference pattern between two sounds of slightly different frequencies, perceived as a periodic variation in volume whose rate is the difference of the two frequencies.

According to the law of superposition, two tones sounding simultaneously are superimposed in a very simple way: one adds their amplitudes. If a graph is drawn to show the function corresponding to the total sound of two strings, it may be seen that maxima and minima are no longer constant as when a pure note is played, but change over time. When the two waves are nearly 180 degrees out of phase the maxima of one wave cancel the minima of the other, whereas when they are nearly in phase their maxima sum up, raising the perceived volume.

Effectively, the high frequency vibrations are added together to generate a much lower frequency vibration. It is important to note that the high frequency vibrations still form the underlying basis of the lower frequency joint vibration. The "beat" frequency that is produced is simply the difference of the two slightly different carrier frequencies: $f_{beat} = f_1 - f_2$.

Let's consider a vibration that has the wavelength of the Planck length. A Planck length is 1.6×10^{-35} meter. A vibrational wave that would have the Planck length as its wavelength would have a frequency of 1.88×10^{43} Hz.

The highest energy gamma rays observed to date in our physical universe come from cosmic sources and have frequencies as high as 10^{28} Hz.

Thus, two vibrational frequencies of 1×10^{43} Hz and $1.000000000000001 \times 10^{43}$ Hz could be added together to obtain a vibrational wave of 10^{28} Hz, and this binaural beat wave would have the same frequency as the highest frequency electromagnetic cosmic rays that are observed in our physical universe. In a similar vein, the lowest electromagnetic frequency that humans can produce are radio waves of 3 Hz. To achieve this frequency would require two vibrational frequencies of 1 x 10^{43} Hz and1.000000000000000000000000000000000000000000000001 x 10^{43} Hz.

So, via a binaural beat mechanism, the ultra-high vibrational frequencies could produce the full range of electromagnetic frequencies observed to date in our physical reality. This means that the Universal Consciousness field would have the ability to produce all of the energy and matter contained in the physical.

The conscious energy frequencies of the Universal Consciousness field are so high that they will have no direct interactions with the physical world. In this respect they are similar to the Dark Matter and Dark Energy that our science tells us exists all around us. Our physical reality is thus contained within Universal Consciousness. Furthermore, since the ultra-high vibrations of Universal Consciousness form the "carrier waves" of the lower frequency physical vibrations, this means that everything in our physical world from photons to electrons on up, contains some level of consciousness, just as is proposed by panpsychism.

Nothing in life is to be feared, it is only to be understood. Now is the time to understand more, so that we may fear less.

Marie Curie

Non-Physical Conscious Entities:

Science says that Dark Matter and Dark Energy pervade everything in our physical universe, but we do not detect them at all with our physical senses or with the scientific equipment that extends our physical senses. It is as if we are intimately within a Dark Universe, and no one knows what may exist in that so-called darkness.

Let us postulate that the Universal Consciousness field is populated by entities that possess both mind and will, just as we human beings do in this physical universe.

Given the Dark Universe that our physical universe exists within, this may be a distinct possibility.

How can a field produce such individualized entities? One analogous way to perceive this is to consider the behavior of a ferrofluid. What is a ferrofluid? A ferrofluid is a liquid that becomes magnetized in the presence of a magnetic field. A ferrofluid is essentially a stable colloidal suspension of nanosized particles that contain iron, such as magnetite or hematite, in a fluid which can be water or some other non-aqueous liquid. Because the magnetic particles are so small and usually stabilized with surfactants, they do not settle out from the liquid, but remain suspended in the liquid in a stable way. Ferrofluids typically appear as black, oily-looking liquids.

If you pour a ferrofluid into a large flat tray, after a short time it will settle down into a flat liquid surface, such as one might see the surface of a lake appearing on a calm summer day. But if you now suspend a strong magnet above the flat surface of the ferrofluid, something remarkable happens. A spike of fluid nucleates from the calm, flat liquid surface and rises from the fluid surface in an attempt to attach itself to the magnet, because the magnetic field of the magnet has magnetized the iron-containing particles in the fluid. This happens because the ferrofluid can lower its energy by a portion of it being in closer physical proximity to the magnet.

So the presence of the magnet causes a distinct, individualized spike to appear, yet this spike continues to be joined at the base to the overall ferrofluid liquid bath. Essentially, an individualized feature has been created from the ferrofluid by the presence of the magnetic field of the magnet above it. If the magnet is taken away, then the individualized spike collapses and returns to the body of the ferrofluid liquid. And the ferrofluid does not retain any residual magnetization when the external magnet is removed.

With ferrofluids and more complex external magnetic fields above them, it is possible to create very beautiful, multiple-faceted structures arising out of the flat liquid that can change, move, and seemingly interact with themselves as the external magnetic fields are varied. Yet the complex three-dimensional structures that are created from the two-dimensional flat ferrofluid surface are still part and parcel of the bulk ferrofluid liquid.

So we can see from this ferrofluid analogy that individualized entities might be derived from an overall field, and that these individualized entities can possess the characteristics of that field.

In order to further explore the possibility of non-physical entities, it is necessary to discuss accounts of the non-physical provided by near-death experiencers since this is the only information available. While such accounts are not strictly scientifically based, there are some which contain veridical evidence that the experiencer's consciousness was remote from the experiencer's physical body at the time of the near-death experience. This veridical evidence provides a significant support to the reality of their reports.

The possibility exists that persons who have had near-death experiences return to our physical world with some conscious knowledge of a non-physical realm. Near-death experiencers report that they experience "beings of light". In fact, they say that their individualized consciousness is now nothing more than conscious "light". Here is the account of one near-death experiencer:

"To describe the experience I floated up to the ceiling where I looked down and saw the medical team dressed in green gowns and caps working seriously over a body. As I observed the process I realized that was the body I had just left. I had no attachment to it whatsoever. Also I had no form; I was like a mist. The next recollection was of floating without effort through a dark tunnel to a beautiful yellow-white light. I had no thought of choosing to go there. It just seemed to naturally draw me to it. I saw no other Beings in the tunnel. In The Light there was only pure beautiful Light. No forms, no boundaries, nothing but beautiful white light. The feeling of peace in the light was like nothing I had ever experienced. There was no such thing as time and space. I refer to me as "I," but I felt no separation. At one point I became all there was. I knew all there was and I had all knowledge. I had a thought and the answer was immediately there. I was the core, the infinite Pure White Light and there was nothing else. I did not like being the only thing there was, and I was lonely.

At some point three Beings of Light, (as I called them), came to me. The middle one seemed to be larger with the two accompanying "it" on each side. Recently I read that every cell has its own frequency or vibration and that frequency has its own tone, therefore our bodies "sing". Perhaps that is how I was able to discern "three" Beings, that they (I, and each of us) have different frequencies, different body tones."

People have long speculated that, at death, our consciousness continues to exist even though the physical brain does not. The reality of this supposition is certainly supported by the veridical near-death experiences that have been reported by many people. In such cases, people say that they could see and hear things that were going on around them, typically in a hospital setting when their brain was medically non-functional.

The most famous and medically well-documented veridical near-death experience is that of Pam Reynolds. Her experience is described in the book "Light and Death" by Dr. Michael Sabom. Pam had a giant basilar artery aneurysm, a ballooned section of a large artery at the base of her brain. If the aneurysm ruptured, the result would be immediate death. So she needed a major operation to fix the problem.

The operation she had in 1991 during which her near-death experience occurred was a very radical one indeed. The surgical team would lower her body temperature to 60° Fahrenheit to induce cardiac arrest, and then drain the blood from her head so that the aneurysm could be safely removed. At the start of the aneurysm removal procedure, she would be quite clinically dead, with no heart beat and no brain waves or brainstem function.

Because this was such a major and radical type of procedure, Pam was extensively monitored during the surgery. Her eyes were taped shut. She had a catheter placed to measure pulmonary pressure and blood flow from the heart. Cardiac monitoring leads were attached to follow heart rate and rhythm, and an oximeter was taped to her index finger to measure oxygen levels in her blood. Urinary temperature was measured by a thermister placed in her bladder and the core body temperature of her inner body was measured with a thermister placed deeply into her esophagus. Her brain temperature was monitored by a thin wire embedded in its surface. She had EEG electrodes taped to her head to record cerebral cortical brain activity, and her auditory nerve center located in the brain stem was tested continuously using 100-decibel clicks at 22 clicks per second (a deep hum as loud as a jackhammer) emitted from small speakers inserted into her ears. In summary, she was fully loaded with instrumentation and diagnostics for the surgery.

Pam was placed under general anesthesia by the anesthesiologist. After ninety minutes of deep anesthesia the surgery began with the surgeon, a Dr. Spetzler, cutting out a large section of Pam's skull with a Midas Rex 73,000 rpm bone saw, which made a loud buzzing noise. Here is Pam's account of what she saw and heard when the operation began:

"The next thing I recall was the sound: It was a natural D. As I listened to the sound, I felt it was pulling me out of the top of my head. The further out of my body I got, the more clear the tone became. I had the impression it was like a road, a frequency that you go on .... I remember seeing several things in the operating room when I was looking down. It was the most aware that I think that I have ever been in my entire life.... I was metaphorically sitting on Dr. Spetzler's shoulder. It was not like normal vision. It was brighter and more focused and clearer than normal vision .... There was so much in the operating room that I didn't recognize, and so many people.

I thought the way they had my head shaved was very peculiar. I expected them to take all of the hair, but they did not ....

The saw thing that I hated the sound of looked like an electric toothbrush and it had a dent in it, a groove at the top where the saw appeared to go into the handle, but it didn't .... And the saw had interchangeable blades, too, but these blades were in what looked like a socket wrench case .... I heard the saw crank up. I didn't see them use it on my head, but I think I heard it being used on something. It was humming at a relatively high pitch and then all of a sudden it went Brrrrrrr! like that.

Someone said something about my veins and arteries being very small. I believe it was a female voice and that it was Dr. Murray, but I'm not sure. She was the cardiologist. I remember thinking that I should have told her about that.... I remember the heart-lung machine. I didn't like the respirator.... I remember a lot of tools and instruments that I did not readily recognize."

After the operation, her surgeon Dr. Spetzler was quite astounded that she was able to describe the things she did, given the fact that she was ninety minutes into deep general anesthesia with her eyes taped shut and loud sounds in her ears. The bone saw that he had used did indeed resemble an electric toothbrush to an uninitiated person. And it did have a set of blades in a case resembling a socket wrench case. The fact is that Pam had never seen such a medical bone saw anytime in her life. And Pam was also able to hear one of the doctors talking about her veins and arteries being small, a conversation that indeed actually took place during the operation. Yet she had plugs in her ears that were giving out 100-decibel clicks like the sound of a jack hammer. She shouldn't have been able to hear a thing. So Pam Reynolds' NDE was dramatically veridical. She was providing proof that her consciousness was outside her body and aware, while her body and brain were deeply anesthetized.

Here is another well-documented veridical near-death experience that was reported in the prestigious medical journal The Lancet (P, van Lommel, et.al., "Near-death experience in survivors of cardiac arrest: a prospective study in the Netherlands", The Lancet, vol. 358, 2039-2045 (2001)). This account was reported by the coronary care unit nurse:

"During a night shift an ambulance brings a 44 year old cyanotic, comatose man into the coronary care unit. He had been found about an hour before in a meadow by passers-by. After admission, he receives artificial respiration without intubation, while heart massage and defibrillation are also applied. When we want to intubate the patient, he turns out to have dentures in his mouth. I remove these upper dentures and put them onto the 'crash cart'. Meanwhile, we continue extensive CPR. After about an hour and a half the patient has sufficient heart rhythm and blood pressure, but he is still ventilated and intubated, and he is still comatose. He is transferred to the intensive care unit to continue the necessary artificial respiration.

Only after more than a week do I meet again with the patient, who is by now back on the cardiac ward. I distribute his medication. The moment he sees me he says: 'Oh, that nurse knows where my dentures are'. I am very surprised. Then he elucidates: 'Yes, you were there when I was brought into hospital and you took my dentures out of my mouth and put them onto that cart, it had all these bottles on it and there was this sliding drawer underneath and there you put my teeth.' I was especially amazed because I remembered this happening while the man was in deep coma and in the process of CPR. When I asked further, it appeared the man had seen himself lying in bed, that he had perceived from above how nurses and doctors had been busy with CPR. He was also able to describe correctly and in detail the small room in which he had been resuscitated as well as the appearance of those present like myself.

At the time that he observed the situation he had been very much afraid that we would stop CPR and that he would die. And it is true that we had been very negative about the patient's prognosis due to his very poor medical condition when admitted. The patient tells me that he desperately and unsuccessfully tried to make it clear to us that he was still alive and that we should continue CPR. He is deeply impressed by his experience and says he is no longer afraid of death. Four weeks later he left the hospital as a healthy man."

The nurse's account was verified via a first-hand interview during which the nurse, identified as T.G., provided the following additional information about the patient (R.H. Smit, "Corroboration of the Dentures Anecdote Involving Veridical Perception in a Near-Death Experience", Journal of Near-Death Studies, vol. 27, no. 1, 47-61 (2008)):

"The patient, B., from Ooy near the city of Nijmegen, had indeed been brought in on a cold night, more dead than alive .... He was clinically dead, period: no heartbeat, no breathing, no blood pressure, and "cold as ice".... immediately after B. entered the hospital, T.G. removed the dentures from B.'s mouth and intubated him before starting up the entire reanimation procedure. Therefore, as T.G. categorically stated, any "normal" observation by the patient of his dentures being removed from his mouth was simply unthinkable.

In addition, the normal observation process could not have been the basis of the patient's detailed description of the crash cart as well as of the entire resuscitation room. Once again, T.G. was adamant in that regard, noting that patient B. had never before been in that hospital, let alone in this resuscitation room, and that this particular crash cart was absolutely unique, being a hand-made product of ramshackle quality that had been stationed in that resuscitation room only and nowhere else. To guess the precise nature of that cart and its contents on the basis of auditory impressions, or through briefly opened eyes characterized by fixed, dilated, unresponsive pupils, was impossible by all accounts. T.G. asserted that certainly it would have been impossible for B. to know precisely where T.G. had placed the dentures."

Perhaps the most astonishing near-death experience with veridical verification reported is that of a Russian man by the name of George Rodonaia. In 1976, Rodonaia, a neuropathologist who was also a Russian dissident and a confirmed atheist, was purposely run over by a car while he was walking on the sidewalk in Moscow. Rodonaia was planning to leave the next day for the United States, and he believed that the KGB wished to kill him before he had a chance to leave the country. They were successful. He was pronounced dead at the scene and his body was taken to a morgue and placed in cold storage for an autopsy that would be performed three days later.

After three days of cold storage, the autopsy was conducted and when the pathologists began cutting into his chest, they were shocked to see him open his eyes and focus his pupils. This was unbelievable to them given that his body had lain for three days in a freezing morgue vault! Rodonaia was immediately transferred to the hospital intensive care unit, and he subsequently spent months recovering from his injuries.

Here is Rodonaia's account of his near-death experience during the three day period his body was declared clinically dead (from the website www.near-death.com/science/evidence/some-people-were-dead-for-several-days.html):

"The first thing I remember about my NDE is that I discovered myself in a realm of total darkness. I had no physical pain, I was still somehow aware of my existence as George, and all about me there was darkness, utter and complete darkness - the greatest darkness ever, darker than any dark, blacker than any black. This was what surrounded me and pressed upon me. I was horrified. I wasn't prepared for this at all. I was shocked to find that I still existed, but I didn't know where I was. The one thought that kept rolling through my mind was, "How can I be when I'm not?" That is what troubled me.

Slowly I got a grip on myself and began to think about what had happened, what was going on. But nothing refreshing or relaxing came to me. Why am I in this darkness? What am I to do? Then I remembered Descartes' famous line: "I think, therefore I am." And that took a huge burden off me, for it was then I knew for certain I was still alive, although obviously in a very different dimension. Then I thought, If I am, why shouldn't I be positive? That is what came to me. I am George and I'm in darkness, but I know I am. I am what I am. I must not be negative.

Then I thought, How can I define what is positive in darkness? Well, positive is light. Then, suddenly, I was in light; bright white, shiny and strong; a very bright light. It was like the flash of a camera, but not flickering - that bright. Constant brightness. At first I found the brilliance of the light painful, I couldn't look directly at it. But little by little I began to relax. I began to feel warm, comforted, and everything suddenly seemed fine.

The next thing that happened was that I saw all these molecules flying around, atoms, protons, neutrons, just flying everywhere. On the one hand, it was totally chaotic, yet what brought me such great joy was that this chaos also had its own symmetry. This symmetry was beautiful and unified and whole, and it flooded me with tremendous joy. I saw the universal form of life and nature laid out before my eyes. It was at this point that any concern I had for my body just slipped away, because it was clear to me that I didn't need it anymore, that it was actually a limitation.

Everything in this experience merged together, so it is difficult for me to put an exact sequence to events. Time as I had known it came to a halt; past, present, and future were somehow fused together for me in the timeless unity of life.

At some point I underwent what has been called the life-review process, for I saw my life from beginning to end all at once. I participated in the real life dramas of my life, almost like a holographic image of my life going on before me - no sense of past, present, or future, just now and the reality of my life. It wasn't as though it started with birth and ran along to my life at the University of Moscow. It all appeared at once. There I was. This was my life. I didn't experience any sense of guilt or remorse for things I'd done. I didn't feel one way or another about my failures, faults, or achievements. All I felt was my life for what it is. And I was content with that. I accepted my life for what it is.

During this time the light just radiated a sense of peace and joy to me. It was very positive. I was so happy to be in the light. And I understood what the light meant. I learned that all the physical rules for human life were nothing when compared to this unitive reality. I also came to see that a black hole is only another part of that infinity which is light.

I came to see that reality is everywhere. That it is not simply the earthly life but the infinite life. Everything is not only connected together, everything is also one. So I felt a wholeness with the light, a sense that all is right with me and the universe.

I could be anywhere instantly, really there. I tried to communicate with the people I saw. Some sensed my presence, but no one did anything about it. I felt it necessary to learn about the Bible and philosophy. You want, you receive. Think and it comes to you. So I participated, I went back and lived in the minds of Jesus and his disciples. I heard their conversations, experienced eating, passing wine, smells, tastes - yet I had no body. I was pure consciousness. If I didn't understand what was happening, an explanation would come. But no teacher spoke. I explored the Roman Empire, Babylon, the times of Noah and Abraham. Any era you can name, I went there."

During Rodonaia's NDE, he went to visit his neighbors who just had a newborn baby that was born just a few days before Rodonaia's "death". This baby would not stop crying and the parents could not understand why. While in the disembodied state, he found that he could communicate with the baby and also "see" inside the baby's body. Here is what Rodonaia said about his interaction with the baby boy:

"I could talk to the baby. It was amazing. I could not talk to the parents - my friends - but I could talk to the little boy who had just been born. I asked him what was wrong. No words were exchanged, but I asked him maybe through telepathy what was wrong. He told me that his arm hurt. And when he told me that, I was able to see that the bone was twisted and broken."

When Rodonaia told his family about being "dead", they did not believe him until he began to provide details about what he saw during his travels out-of-body. Then they became much less skeptical. He told his neighbors about "visiting" them that night and of their concern over their new child. He told them that he had "talked" to the baby and discovered that the baby had a greenstick fracture of its arm which had happened when its body became twisted during its birth. The parents took the child to a doctor who x-rayed the arm and discovered that this was indeed the case.

The above veridical near-death experiences are indicative that your consciousness, your mind with its will and intent, survives physical death and transfers itself to a non-physical reality where it continues to exist as a non-physical entity.

There are almost no scientific experiments related to the continued existence of consciousness after death. However, one interesting experiment has been conducted by Prof. Gary Schwartz, the Director of the Laboratory for Advances in Consciousness and Health at the University of Arizona (here is the published reference: Gary E. Schwartz, "Possible Application of Silicon Photomultiplier Technology to Detect the Presence of Spirit and Intention: Three Proof-of-Concept Experiments", Explore, vol. 6, 166-171 (2010)).

In this experiment, a state-of-the-art silicon photomultiplier system was employed to detect low photon levels potentially associated with the presence of a non-physical (i.e. spirit) entity. The photomultiplier system employed was quite sophisticated and sensitive to extremely low photon levels. It was able to distinguish the impingement of individual photons on the detector.

Sums of numbers of photons (counted over approximately 90-millisecond time periods (i.e. approximately 12 time periods per second) were displayed and stored by using integrating software. Photon sums per 90 millisecond time period could range from 0 (no photons detected within a given period) to 10,800,000 (the maximum number within a given period displayed by the software).

The photomultiplier system was placed in a very light-tight "box within a box within a box" environment to minimize any ambient light from reaching the photomultiplier from outside the box environment. With this arrangement, the background light was reduced to less than an average of a total of only three photon sums greater than 0 collected over five minutes; each sum contained approximately 13 to 25 individual photon counts. So this photon detection system was very, very sensitive to the presence of light photons.

Non-physical (i.e. spirit) entities were invited to participate in the experiments by the experimenter. These spirit participants had all been involved to various degrees in previous mediumship research and four research mediums independently claimed that these hypothesized spirits were committed to the photomultiplier research, and would listen for mental requests from the experimenter to be present and follow the procedures as requested.

The results of this investigation are quite intriguing. Statistically significant larger quantities of photons were detected by the photomultiplier when the spirits were "present" than when they were "not present". Detected photons were higher in the presence of the spirits than those of control experiments with no spirits invited to participate. Care was taken to rule out any potential effects that might have resulted from the intention of the experimenter.

What are we to make of these experimental results? They appear to suggest that non-physical entities can interact with the physical through the appearance of unaccounted-for increased quantities of photons. The experiments just described are the first ever performed to attempt to quantify a link between the physical and the non-physical. They certainly suggest the need and importance of further experimentation along these lines.

What is it like to be a non-physical entity, a "being of light" if you will. Well, one might start by asking the question: What is it like to be a photon? A photon has no mass and no charge. It travels in our spacetime at the speed of light, so according to Einstein's general relativity, it experiences no space and no time. Thus, non-physical entities do not reside in spacetime, but in "something" that is outside of it.

Perhaps non-physical entities can be thought of as distinct little packets of the consciousness vibratory energy that is the Universal Consciousness Field. As is the case with the ferrofluid analogy, these entities may appear as distinct separate entities, yet they are intimately joined to the overall Field and are composed of the same essence. They are little bits of vibratory consciousness energy.

Now I know you will be saying to yourself: How can energy possess the attributes of mind and will? The energy that we experience here in the physical certainly seems as though it is completely unconscious in the way that it produces "work" on the external environment. Under a given set of initial conditions, physical energy always induces the same final outcome. There seems to be no mind or will aspect to it at all.

Yes, that is how we perceive energy in the physical, as a mindless ability to do work. Yet the mind and will that we know we have must come from somewhere, and the most likely somewhere is the non-physical, which we hypothesize as an all-encompassing Universal Consciousness Field. Following along this line, logic would dictate that the Universal Consciousness Field itself possesses both mind and will, but on a grand scale completely unfathomable to our understanding here in the physical. The Universal Consciousness Field is vibratory conscious energy, a much more fundamental and complex form of energy which underlies the energy that we experience in the physical realm.

Let us postulate that the non-physical is composed of different "levels". Each of these levels (you can call them different dimensions if you like) are separated on the basis of their consciousness vibrational levels.

I have no idea how many non-physical levels there might be. But my intuition is that all these non-physical levels, as well as our physical spacetime level, are all contained as subsets of the overall Universal Consciousness Field. In other words, All is One.

The entities that exist in each of these levels have different consciousness vibrational frequency ranges. One can think of this as analogous to the different frequency ranges of the electromagnetic spectrum. There are extremely low frequencies, low frequencies, radio waves, microwaves, infrared, visible light, ultraviolet, x-rays, and finally gamma rays.

Entities at a given consciousness frequency level have unimpeded access to all levels that are below them, but they have only limited access to levels higher than their own. One can think of this in the following way. Consider that you are midway along a steeply inclined path. It is easy for you to walk down the path and you may perceive that as you walk downward it gets darker and darker but you are still able to walk down. But if you try to walk up the steeply inclined path, it is much more difficult to do so and you perceive that it gets brighter and brighter as you ascend. Finally, you reach a point where you cannot proceed any further because the brightness is just too intense. While interactions between two adjacent consciousness frequency levels may be relatively easy, interactions with higher levels are not.

In order for an entity to access lower consciousness frequency levels, it would be necessary for the entity to lower its consciousness vibrational level. This might be done via the beat frequency methodology that was discussed previously, using differential carrier frequencies that are available within the entity's natural frequency range.

One might ask: How can a non-physical entity move up to reside at a higher consciousness frequency level? This is a more difficult question. There should be a mechanism to increase consciousness vibrational frequency, just as there is an analogy binaural beat mechanism to decrease consciousness vibrational frequency. However, it is more difficult because increasing the consciousness vibrational frequency requires that its carrier fundamental frequency level be actually increased.

According to our present physics, there are only a very limited number of ways that the frequency of a photon traveling in the vacuum free space (i.e. a photon that has already been emitted from a source) can be changed. These are called “red shift” (a decrease in frequency) and “blue shift” (an increase in frequency).

The first way this can happen is through the relative velocities of the source where the photon is emitted and the location where the photon is detected. This is termed the Doppler shift, and is only large enough to be observed on the cosmological scale. When the emitting source is moving away from the Earth, the photons that it emits are reduced in frequency. If the emitting source is moving towards the Earth, the photons that it emits are increased in frequency. Such decreases or increases are typically detected through spectral line shifts in elements such as hydrogen.

While the light from most of the observable galaxies in the universe is red shifted because they are moving away from us, there are exceptions in our local group of galaxies. Such an exception is the Andromeda galaxy which is 2.5 million light years from Earth. The light from the Andromeda galaxy is actually blue shifted, so Andromeda is known to be moving towards our Milky Way galaxy. Similarly, the light from Barnard’s star, 6 light years from Earth, is blue shifted because it is moving towards our sun.

The second way to change the frequency of a traveling photon is related to the observed expansion of the universe. As first detected by astronomer Edwin Hubble in 1929, the light from objects in the universe is overwhelmingly red shifted, and the amount of this red shift increases with increasing distance from the Earth. This observed red shift is taken to mean that the space of the universe is itself expanding and because of this the wavelengths of any photons in space are increasing and thus their frequencies are decreasing. This is called the cosmological red shift. There is no observed cosmological blue shift because for that to happen, the universe would have to be contracting and getting smaller.

The third way the frequency of a photon can be changed is through gravitational effects. Photons generated from a high gravitational field object become less energetic and thus are red shifted when observed in a lower gravitational field frame of reference. Similarly, photons originating from a low gravitation field location exhibit a blue shift when viewed from a higher gravitational field reference frame. These are effects related to gravitational time dilation in Einstein's general theory of relativity.

It seems unlikely that any of the above mechanisms are associated with raising the frequency level of the consciousness vibrational frequency. Since the consciousness frequency is postulated to be related to consciousness energy in more or less the same way that electromagnetic frequency is related to electromagnetic energy, if by some means energy is added to the consciousness vibration, then its frequency should increase. But how such energy might be added is a mystery.

If there are different levels of the non-physical, then it would be logical that there are different levels of entities that reside within them. We know of the physical entities that reside in our level of three-dimensional spacetime, but what about non-physical entities.

One might conjecture that the next level above our three-dimensional subset of reality is the level that near-death experiencers report. According to their accounts, this level is inhabited by beings composed of "light" who communicate with them in a nonverbal way. They report intense light that does not hurt their non-physical "eyes". They often describe themselves as being a conscious "point of light". They report higher levels of awareness and perceptual clarity, and often ranges of colors that are larger and more dramatic than can be experienced in the physical. If they think of being at another location, they are instantaneously there. In life reviews, they report the experiencing of past events as if these past events were actually happening in the "Now". They often report knowing all knowledge and feeling an interconnectedness with everything that exists. The near-death experiencers also report feeling the presence of and interacting with beings that they feel are of higher levels.

Here I think it is important to state the following. The possibility exists that the consciousness essence of a physical human being, the "I", is in actuality a non-physical entity that has lowered its consciousness vibrational energy in order to experience the physical level of reality. Essentially, this non-physical entity is the

"ghost in the physical machine" and it is what constitutes your mind and will.

The notion that science and spirituality are somehow mutually exclusive does a disservice to both.

Carl Sagan

The Universal Consciousness Field:

We have now come to the end of our exploration of the physics of the non-physical. It has been postulated that the overarching fundamental of both physical and non-physical reality is the Universal Consciousness Field. This Field permeates everything in the physical, from subatomic particles to the vast galaxies of the visible universe, as well as the portion of the physical universe that we are not able to observe from our Earthly vantage point. Your physical body is immersed in the Universal Consciousness Field.

Your mind, which is non-physical in nature, is also a part of the Universal Consciousness Field. In fact, You, your consciousness essence, is a portion of this Field. You are fundamentally a little bit of consciousness vibratory energy.

You are not separate from the Universal Consciousness Field. While it seems in the physical that you are a separate entity, in fact you are intimately connected to the Field, just as the spikes in a ferrofluid are intimately connected to the bulk of the ferrofluid.

Reality consists of a number of consciousness frequency levels, of which the physical is the lowest level. However, all of these levels are contained as subsets within the Universal Consciousness Field, and transition between levels occurs.

Finally, what is the Universal Conscious Field? Fundamentally, the Universal Consciousness Field is the only Being that truly exists.

Everything else, both physical and non-physical, is a manifestation of the Universal Consciousness Field.

The Universal Consciousness Field is All That Is.

About the Author:

Dr. John Joseph Petrovic is a scientist who retired from the Los Alamos National Laboratory as a Laboratory Fellow in 2005 after thirty-three years of scientific research in many areas of materials science. He has published two hundred scientific papers and holds ten U.S. patents.

Since his retirement, he has been actively seeking to understand the nature of reality and spirituality, by combining his scientific perspective with his personal intuition. To date, he has published five books on these topics:

"The First Principles: A Scientist's Guide to the Spiritual" (c. 2008, John Joseph Petrovic)

"Exploring Death: What You Should Know About Dying" (c. 2010, John Joseph Petrovic)

"Dreams of Reality" (c. 2012, John Joseph Petrovic)

"The God Within" (c. 2016, John Joseph Petrovic)

"Physics of the Non-Physical" (c. 2018, John Joseph Petrovic)

11178551R00087

Printed in Great Britain
by Amazon